2018 *Fauquier Community Read*
Selection for Younger Readers
Provided
By
Friends of the Fauquier Library

RUNNING WITH ROSELLE

RUNNING WITH ROSELLE

HOW A BLIND BOY AND A PUPPY
GREW UP, BECAME BEST FRIENDS,
AND TOGETHER SURVIVED
ONE OF AMERICA'S DARKEST DAYS

MICHAEL HINGSON
with Jeanette Hanscome

Roselle's Dream Foundation
Novato, California

Published in Novato, California by Roselle's Dream
Foundation.

ISBN   0615905234
ISBN13   978-0615905235

Note to Readers

Running with Roselle is a true story. Some names have
been changed. We also fictionalized some dialogue,
dramatic details, and scenes for the sake of creating
engaging snapshots into Mike's growing-up years,
Roselle's training, and their experiences together. Each
scene was reviewed by someone who lived it, and we
made every effort to present people in a realistic and
respectful light.

DEDICATION

This book is dedicated to the very special people in
Roselle's and my life who gave us the skills
and knowledge to live life to the fullest
and to survive whatever comes along.
This book is especially dedicated to
some incredible and special teachers.
—Mike

To my sons Christian and Nathan,
my sisters Sherry and Kristy,
and my parents Frank and Beverly La Chapell—
Thank you for treating this exciting project
like a family event, and for loving Roselle
as much as I did.
—Jeanette

CONTENTS

EXTRAS

SEPTEMBER 11, 2001

Mike Hingson sniffed the air of his 78th-floor office. The ham and cheese croissant sandwiches he'd just set out for his guests made his stomach growl.

His yellow Labrador retriever, Roselle, snoozed under his desk with her head on his feet, her favorite pillow. A guide dog, Roselle went everywhere with Mike, including to his office at the World Trade Center in New York City.

He gently pulled his feet out from under Roselle's head. She let out a loud snore. He didn't even have time to laugh before a thunderous boom made him gasp instead. The building leaned to one side, almost knocking him off his feet. His heart leapt in his chest.

"What was that?"

Mike grabbed the side of the table as the tower tipped even more. Glass shattered. Metal creaked.

Roselle let out another snore. Since the day they met at Guide Dogs for the Blind almost two years ago, Roselle and Mike had been constant companions. But today, his life would depend on his unusual bond with the golden dog under his desk.

Part 1: Growing Up Separately

1

PUPPY SCHOOL

Roselle, 1998

Roselle snatched a rubber ring off the grass and took off running. Her sister, Renna, chased her through a long tube-shaped play tunnel. A black puppy met them on the other side, tail wagging, ready to pounce. Roselle bowled him over and kept running with her ring, gripping it in her jaws so no one could steal it back.

This group of yellow and black Labradors, golden retrievers, and Lab-retriever mixes might have looked like ordinary puppies with access to a very elaborate, well-stocked playground, but Roselle and her kennel mates were actually in training. Playtime—or socialization, as the staff called it—was part of their daily routine.

Roselle and the other puppies had been born in empty plastic kiddie pools, in the whelping room at Guide Dogs for the Blind in San Rafael, California. Since before they were born, everything about their lives had been carefully planned, right down to which breeds were best suited to guide blind people. Roselle and her littermates, who popped into the world on March 12, 1998, had names beginning with R to keep them from getting mixed up with other litters. Because no two guide dogs either working or training could have the same name, they needed to be unusual. Roselle's litter included her sister. Renna. and her three brothers, Reece, Rollo, and Romeo.

During their first few weeks of life, the puppies had been watched, fed, named, and marked, first with a tiny shave mark on the shoulder and later with a tattoo on the ear made from green vegetable dye.

Roselle had grown like crazy in the eight weeks since she squirmed into the world of Guide Dogs for the Blind as a little sunshine-yellow butterball. The bigger and stronger she got, the more fun she had chasing her brothers, sister, and friends.

Roselle ran to the middle of the grass and dropped to her tummy to get a tighter grip on the ring. The green identification mark on her ear blurred as she shook the toy and let out a playful growl. Out of nowhere, the black Lab leapt onto Roselle's back. The two puppies rolled in a tangle of black and yellow then leapt to their feet.

A group of children standing outside the pen laughed.

"Aw, look at them." A little girl leaned over the edge of the pen for a better view. She reached out, her fingers wriggling in the air.

"Can we pet them, please?" A curly-haired boy in a hooded sweatshirt clasped his hands and jumped up and down.

"You've been a good group. I think we can trust you to pet a puppy." The lady in charge of their tour asked a gray-haired man to fetch one of the puppies.

He scooped up Roselle and walked to a bench, settling her in his lap. Roselle panted with anticipation. The puppies had grown accustomed to regular visits from children on field trips, writers doing research, or ordinary families who were interested in knowing more about this place called Guide Dogs for the Blind.

"This is Roselle." The tour guide stroked her soft, freshly washed coat.

"Gently," the children's teacher warned. "One at a time. Form a line, please."

"She's so cute." A girl with cold hands stroked Roselle's back then her silky ears. "Hi, Roselle."

Roselle nestled into each stroke and pat, soaking up the affection. She squirmed with joy.

"Calm down, shh." The gray-haired man whispered

to the puppy as he got a tighter grip. Then he turned to the children. "This little one loves visitors."

"Isn't all this attention overwhelming for the puppies?" the teacher asked.

"It's actually good for them." The man turned Roselle around to face the whole group. "These puppies need to get used to all kinds of situations, including strangers touching them."

Another girl took one of Roselle's front paws. "Can you shake?" She examined it more closely. "Hey, look, she has webbed feet."

"That's right," the tour guide said. "Labs have webbed feet like a duck. That's what makes them such good swimmers. Not that she'll do much swimming as a guide dog."

An enticing smell drew Roselle's attention away from the girl. A little boy was rubbing under her chin, and his hand smelled like something good to eat. She licked it.

"Roselle, no." The man pulled her back.

Roselle looked at the boy, saying sorry with her large, chocolate brown eyes. Hearing "Roselle, no" made the sweet-salty taste from the boy's hand turn sour.

"Must be the ham from my sandwich."

"Try again," the tour guide told the boy.

This time when the boy's ham-scented hand stroked Roselle's chin, she forced her tongue to stay in her mouth.

"Good girl, Roselle," the woman praised. "Good."

Good girl. Roselle wagged her tail. I did good.

She patted Roselle's head. "Guide dog puppies are taught that licking is inappropriate behavior."

"But don't all dogs lick?" a boy asked. "My dog licks me awake almost every morning."

"These are special puppies. If they pass all of their training, they'll have a job to do. Licking, chewing, and other distractions keep them from focusing on the blind person they are supposed to keep safe." The man stood. "Tomorrow is an exciting day for Roselle. She gets to leave campus and meet her puppy raisers."

Leave? Roselle's ears pricked. But I like it here.

"They get to keep her? Lucky!"

"Yes, but only for a little while. They must return her after a year, which is always hard. While Roselle is with her raisers, she will learn important skills that get her ready for guide dog training."

The tour guide looked at her watch. "Okay, it's time to say goodbye to Roselle and continue with our tour."

"Bye, Roselle." The last little girl stroked her back before following the class.

"Bye, Roselle," the children called as they walked away. "Have a good day in puppy school."

The man waved Roselle's paw. Roselle watched

the children walk away. *Too bad they couldn't stay longer to play. Play is my favorite part of the day.*

"I'm going to ask my mom if we can raise a guide dog puppy," one little boy told his teacher.

The man set Roselle back in the play area. "Just a few more minutes, then it's time for a walk."

Ten minutes later, Roselle was on her leash, walking a sunny path with several other puppies and volunteers. When Roselle sniffed the grass, her volunteer tugged her leash as a correction, praising her when she immediately stepped back in line. Even though her natural instinct as a dog was to sniff everything around her, she needed to learn to look ahead.

The parade of puppies and walkers circled the path then passed the stage where graduations were held after guide dog training courses. Only 50 percent of the puppies would graduate.

Roselle's walker directed her to a small flight of steps. Roselle's little legs faltered on the second step, but she quickly regained her balance and bounced her way up all five steps. Then it was time to go down. Roselle hesitated at the top. *Down is scary.*

But when the puppy walker headed down, Roselle hopped down one step, then the next, until she'd conquered all of the steps.

"Good girl, Roselle." The lady patted Roselle's head. "Going down is hard."

The other puppies followed. Roselle's brother Romeo tripped on the last step and toppled in a little yellow heap before picking himself up again.

"Oops." Romeo's walker helped him get his leg untangled from the leash. "You'll learn."

Roselle slept in her kennel with her brothers and sister that night, tired from a full day. She awoke to sunshine and a bowl of puppy kibble blended especially for her by the experts in the kennel kitchen. Today, instead of going to the play area, Roselle and her brother Reece were carried to a specially modified van with a big picture of a yellow Lab on it, known as the Puppy Truck. Some of the other puppies, like her sister Renna, didn't go in the truck. Instead, their puppy raisers would drive to campus to pick them up. Roselle had heard someone say that Renna was going to a family from Carson City, Nevada.

A volunteer gently coaxed Roselle into a blanket-lined carrier. She only squealed once before nestling down with her face between her paws, looking up at the man as he shut the latch then settled Reece into his carrier.

"We'll miss you too, girl. But you have a family waiting for you in Santa Barbara."

Mick, the driver, secured the two carriers before reaching for a third puppy. "Those puppy-raising clubs make a big deal about delivery day. You'll be regular celebrities."

Roselle popped her head up. Mick patted the top of her carrier and shut the door. *Being a celebrity sounds like a good thing, but will it always feel this scary?*

2

LEARNING TO HEAR THE COFFEE TABLE

Mike, 1954

"Vroom!" Mike gripped the steering wheel and placed his feet firmly on the pedals of the kid-sized car. "Vroom, vroom, vroom!"

Pushing with his right foot then his left, he drove forward, picking up speed as the wheels made that wonderful swoosh sound over the hardwood floor of his family's Chicago apartment. Around the living room he sped, past Dad's chair on the right and the table beside it.

He heard the announcer in his head. *And it's Michael 'the Blizzard' Hingson in the lead! He's coming into the final lap!*

Blizzard was Mike's real middle name. His parents chose it because he'd been born during a horrible blizzard on February 24, 1950. But today the only blizzard was Mike, whipping around the living room like the Chicago wind.

He's coming up to the finish line. He's . . .

Crash!

Mike's chin hit the coffee table with a cruel smack. He reached up and felt the smooth wood in front of him. He'd forgotten about the coffee table. Mike's lip trembled and his eyes filled with tears as the pain set in. He let out a howl, gripping his chin. *Dumb coffee table!* Mike wanted to yell or smack it or both. It was just tall enough for the hood of the pedal car to zoom under, but not nearly tall enough for the four-year-old driver.

"Mom!" His six-year-old brother Ellery ran to the kitchen. "Come quick!"

Sarah Hingson rushed in.

"Mike, Honey?" Mike felt his mother's gentle arms encircle him, coaxing him out of the car. "Oh no, you're bleeding."

A couple of hours later, Mike sat in the backseat of a taxi, using a finger to trace the bandage covering three stitches in his chin. He waited for Mom to break her silence and scold him for racing so fast indoors or for Dad to say they needed to take the pedal car away for a while. The thought of losing his

22

pedal car hurt more than the stitches.

Ellery sat beside him. *Will they give my car to Ellery?*

"Michael," Mom said.

He waited for the bad news.

"You need to do a better job of watching where you're going."

Mike straightened up. The weight of dread lifted. *That's it? Just watch where I'm going? I can do that, easy!*

Some might consider this a strange thing to say to a four-year-old who had been blind since shortly after birth. But Mike knew exactly what his mother meant. He needed to learn to listen better.

For as long as Mike could remember, his world had been dark. Blind, people called it. Ellery could see; so could his parents. Mike had heard Mom and Dad share his story with other adults many times—how he'd been born two months early and put in an incubator with high levels of oxygen, which damaged his eyes and blinded him forever. At first they thought he might have a cataract because one eye looked cloudy. Then came the day when his Aunt Shirley was babysitting him and the morning sun poured in through the kitchen window. Aunt Shirley scooped up baby Mike and rushed over to shut the blinds, only to discover that his pale blue eyes were wide open. He didn't squint or fuss in the bright light.

Aunt Shirley had to tell Mike's mom, "I don't think he can see."

When the doctor confirmed Mike's blindness and decided nothing could be done, he encouraged Mike's parents to send him to a special home for people with disabilities.

"He'll never be able to do anything on his own. If you try to raise him at home, he'll only be a burden."

But they refused to send their little boy away.

His parents cried at the news. All the relatives cried. But nobody cried about it anymore or even acted like being blind was a bad thing.

Mike knew that blind made him different, but a burden? He'd never been treated like one. And he did plenty of things on his own. His parents expected the same things from him that they expected from Ellery. He had to clean his room like Ellery, was expected to obey and do chores, and if he ran into something, he needed to learn to watch where he was going, just like Ellery. Ellery did this by paying closer attention with his eyes. Mike watched where he was going by using his ears. The day after the pedal car crash, Mike was behind the wheel once again, this time listening for the vibrations of the coffee table.

Mrs. Hingson encouraged her active boys to play outside as much as possible, so Mike learned to watch where he was going while keeping up with Ellery in the neighborhood. Aunt Ruth and Uncle Sam lived in the apartment right beside Mike's, with their two children, Steve and Robin. Uncle Abe and Aunt Shirley, who also lived nearby, had Holly and Dava. Mike always had a playmate, not that any of them felt the need to be extra careful with him just because he couldn't see.

Outside with Ellery and his cousins, Mike watched where he was going with the help of little clicking sounds that he made with his mouth. No one taught him how to do it. He just tried it one day. As he clicked his tongue, he listened for the vibrations of things that might jump out of nowhere and trip him up, like trees and fences. Empty space sounded one way and a parked car sounded another way.

"You sound like a bat," his brother Ellery teased one afternoon as they played.

Mike didn't realize he really was using echolocation, just like a bat. *I'm just watching where I'm going like Mom said to do.*

Mike often walked to the candy store with Ellery and the cousins to buy his favorite treat: penny pretzel sticks and orange soda. At first his cousin Robin held his hand, but eventually he kept up with the pack on his own. Some days he took the lead. Pretzels and soda were worth running ahead for.

When he wasn't playing with Ellery and his cousins, Mike enjoyed tagging along with his father, who had a television repair business. Those were the days when TV's were still a relatively new invention. They also cost a lot of money, so if a problem came up, customers were willing to pay someone to fix it. One morning Mike stood back while his father worked on a television. He listened to the taps and grinds of Dad's tools. What did the inside of a television feel like? Probably pretty neat. Mike couldn't help himself. He reached out a hand. Just as his fingers met a thin wire, an awful zap sent a painful buzz through his hand and arm.

Mike fell to the floor, too shocked to cry.

He felt the weight of his father's stare.

"Sorry, Dad."

Dad pulled him up. "Are you hurt?" He checked Mike's hand.

Mike expected to be punished. After all, he had interfered in Dad's work. Instead, Dad sat him down. "I think it's time for a lesson in basic electricity."

George Hingson gave Mike a lesson in how to stay safe around live circuits and avoid getting shocked again—the first of many science lessons.

But the day soon came when Mike would need more than hands-on science tips from Dad. He was old enough for kindergarten and Mr. and Mrs. Hingson needed to decide where Mike would go to school. Although they stood firm in their choice not to send Mike away to a school for the blind, they did want him to learn to read and write. That meant learning Braille. How could he learn Braille in a regular kindergarten classroom?

"There are other parents of blind children in the area," Mike overheard Mom tell Dad one night after supper. "If we push hard enough, maybe we can get the school to hire a Braille teacher."

"It's worth a try," Dad said.

That fall, Mike started kindergarten at Perry Elementary, the local public school in a class especially for blind children. Many of his ten classmates had also been preemies and gone blind from the oxygen in their incubators.

On the first day, a teacher with special training in working with blind children introduced Mike and the rest of the children to a thick sheet of paper covered in raised dots.

"Each dot or combination of dots is a letter or number," she explained.

She walked around the room and placed each child's fingertips on the sheet so they could feel the single, raised dot that represented the letter "A."

Mike's fingers brushed over the little bump. *This is an A? Wow!*

Later she showed him the machine that made Braille letters and numbers, called a Braillewriter. *I can't wait to learn how to use it. That machine is almost as amazing as my pedal car. Almost.*

3

PUPPY IN TRAINING

Roselle, 1998

Abump shook the truck and woke Roselle from her nap. She raised her head as the Puppy Truck slowed and came to a stop. Reece let out a bark. Roselle answered it, triggering a chain reaction of happy yelps. *Finally. Time to get out!*

"They're here." The announcement came from someone outside.

Mick shut off the engine. They'd arrived at the Santa Barbara County Sightseers, a club for people raising guide dog puppies. Those receiving new puppies waited outside under the traditional cloud of mystery, knowing nothing about their dog except its first initial.

Cheers and claps rang out when the driver opened

the van door.

"I've been trying to guess my puppy's name all week," one lady said.

Sunlight poured in. Roselle stood erect, her tail swishing. She pressed her nose against the wire cage of her carrier. *Who out there belongs to me?*

"Are you ready to meet your new friend?" Mick asked the group.

The claps told Roselle they were definitely ready.

Mick climbed back into the truck and picked up a clipboard. The small group got quiet except for a few scattered whispers.

Mick kneeled down to open Roselle's carrier. He smiled as he lifted her out into the fresh air of Santa Barbara, California. Her heart fluttered with excitement and nerves. The group was small, but all were strangers to Roselle. Most of the people had dogs with them, wearing smaller versions of the coats that Roselle had seen on dogs at the Guide Dogs for the Blind campus. One family stood near the back and looked sad.

"Holly Cline," Mick called. He rubbed Roselle's head. "Here's your new girl. Meet Roselle."

A pretty lady with long blond hair put her hands up to Roselle's face, smiling at Roselle and then at the people around her. "This never stops being fun."

Holly wrapped her arms around Roselle, hugging her as if they would be a family forever. "Oh,

Sweetie, you're trembling." Holly held her closer. "What a cutie!"

The lady beside Holly reached out and squeezed Roselle's paw. "I love how their paws are still too big for their bodies."

Mick reached back into the truck and pulled out a bag. "Here is Roselle's ID tag, collar, puppy vest, and other things. Like I need to tell you, Holly. You're an old pro at this."

Roselle wiggled against Holly's gentle embrace. After spending so many hours in the truck, Roselle longed to get down and run. But Holly kept her in her arms, tightening her hold and calming her with a back rub. Until they had all their immunizations, guide dog puppies could only be set down in their raiser's home or backyard to roam.

Mick read his clipboard again. "It looks like I have a pick-up as well."

"That's us." The family that Roselle had spotted earlier approached the van with their dog. They all looked ready to cry.

"It's always hard to send you guys back," Holly told Roselle. "But going back means you are ready for formal training, and that's a good thing."

A boy of about twelve wiped away tears as he watched his dog climb into the van with Mick.

His mom sniffed. "We're already signed up for another puppy."

Holly touched the woman's arm. "That's the only thing that makes saying goodbye tolerable—knowing we can do it again."

The van pulled away with Reece still inside. He was going to a different club.

Holly held Roselle close as people moved in close and snapped pictures. Holly's gentle voice and touch helped Roselle relax. Roselle kept her eyes on Holly as she was passed around and cuddled by other families in the Sightseers club. The older puppies sat or lay in the down position, waiting patiently.

A man passing by stopped to watch. "Wow, I teach obedience classes and have never seen anything like this. Not one of your dogs is barking, whining, or getting up. How did you make that happen? Sedatives?"

"Well, they work hard to become this obedient."

"I need to start getting my tips from guide dog trainers."

"Visit anytime."

Everyone laughed. Each member of Sightseers had gone through a lengthy process before receiving their first puppy—attending club meetings, filling out an application, being interviewed, having their home and yard inspected, and puppy-sitting as practice. They accepted each new puppy knowing that the adorable bundle did not belong to them but to Guide Dogs for the Blind in San Rafael, California. They understood their job: to train and socialize a well-behaved dog until he or she was old enough to return to campus for formal training. Some raisers had started as teenagers fulfilling a community service requirement, while others were retired couples. Some families simply adored dogs and the idea of preparing one for such a great purpose. Even with the sad goodbyes, they took on puppy after puppy. Holly was on her fourth.

The rest of the day was a blur of voices and snuggles and up-close smiles and another car trip, this time to Holly's house, where Roselle finally got to get down and explore. Holly placed her food and water dishes in a special place, showed Roselle where she would sleep then took her outside to relieve, waiting quietly and patiently as Roselle did her "business," as the trainers called it. Even at such a young age, she was learning to do this on command. The goal was to have her do it only on command.

Afterward, Holly let Roselle run around the backyard for a while. Roselle found a puppy-sized chew toy and immediately leapt on it. How strange to play alone instead of with my friends. But as soon as she started missing her old friends, Holly sat on the grass, grabbed the toy, and started a game of fetch. When Roselle ran back with the bone-shaped toy, Holly caught her in her lap and gave her a hug before tossing the bone again. Playing with Holly wasn't like playing with other puppies, but it was the next best thing.

Then it was time to eat. Holly placed Roselle beside her dish then gently pushed on her bottom. "Roselle, sit."

Roselle sat.

"Good girl. Now, wait."

Roselle remained sitting while Holly poured the right amount of food into her dish. She panted, her mouth watering for the kibble. Her body twitched with her desire to dive into the food, but she waited. *I can do this.* Holly's kindness made it easier to obey.

Finally, Holly said, "Okay," releasing Roselle to eat.

Next, they did the same with her water. Soon, it was time for bed. Roselle curled up, full and tired. What a long day.

Roselle woke up to a new life with Holly, who took her to a lot of interesting places. Some areas like crowded stores were too overwhelming at first, so they stood back, getting Roselle accustomed to the noise of shoppers, crying toddlers, and voices over loudspeakers. She learned very quickly that the green vest-like coat marked "Guide Dog Puppy in Training" meant she was working. Roselle also discovered that the vest earned her a lot of attention. While other dogs had to stay outside, she got to go through the door. Passers-by greeted Roselle like she was important. Some had to be told not to pet her, especially children.

"Sorry, this puppy is in training right now," Holly would say, always politely.

As much as Roselle enjoyed meeting new people, she needed to learn to focus.

Back at Holly's house, free of the coat, she could play just like any other puppy.

The first week flew by. The night of the next countywide Sightseers meeting, Holly dressed Roselle in her coat and acted especially excited.

"You get introduced tonight," Holly said as they got in the car.

Introduced? What does that mean?

Roselle learned the meaning when Holly was called up front at the beginning of the meeting.

Holly faced the group of people and dogs. "My new puppy's name is Roselle."

The men and women cheered, still clapping as they formed a circle around Holly and Roselle. Before she knew it, Roselle was being passed from one person to another, each member taking a turn welcoming her to the club.

The next big outing wasn't nearly as fun.

"Time to go to the vet." Holly sounded as if they were going out to play.

Roselle had learned the word *vet* a long time ago,

and that the vet usually involved pain. If she hadn't been learning not to whine, she would have squealed the whole way there.

"Another future guide dog, Holly?" the vet asked once they were there. He rubbed Roselle's face and smiled at her as she sniffed the cold metal table. It smelled like other dogs. Scared dogs. She knew he was trying to calm her down before sticking her with the needle, but it didn't work. She'd been poked enough times to know that nothing could make up for what was coming. Nothing.

"What can I say?" Holly tickled Roselle's chin. "I'm hooked."

The scent of Holly's hand and her touch calmed her.

"I can see why." He rubbed Roselle's back. He reached into his pocket. "Hey, Roselle." He felt around for a chunky part of her hip. "Yeah, that's a good girl. You're a pretty girl."

Pretty? Pretty is good. Maybe this man isn't so bad after all.

The prick of the needle brought an immediate yelp. The medicine stung and her hip felt hot. She tried to squirm out the vet's grip. The traitor.

"I'm sorry. I know. I'd be mad at me, too."

Holly rubbed Roselle's ears and back. "It's all over. If you were my child, I'd buy you ice cream or a toy."

By evening, even ice cream wouldn't have made

Roselle feel better. She lay on Holly's lap feeling miserable, her face puffed up, supposedly a reaction from that horrible shot.

"You poor thing." Holly massaged her fur, speaking softly to her. "The vet said this happens sometimes. You're going to be okay. Although you do look pretty pitiful."

Holly kept her home until the swelling went down, watching her constantly.

♥ 🐈 ♥ 🐈 ♥

Roselle learned to love her new house and Holly just in time to discover that this wasn't her home after all. Holly was only a starter trainer who took puppies until they were immunized. Holly drove her to another house in a town called Montecito, where a nice looking couple met them at the door. Their names were Ted and Kay Stern, and Roselle would stay with them for the rest of her year of puppy training.

"Oh, she's adorable." Kay reached out to Roselle, who sniffed her hand and nudged closer.

Holly stroked Roselle's face. "I'll miss you so much."

Kay pressed her nose against Roselle's neck. "That smell." She breathed in deeply. "She smells so sweet. It's almost intoxicating."

"Told you." Holly gave Roselle a sad smile.

"Ted, smell her fur."

He reached out and rubbed Roselle's neck. "I'll take your word for it, Honey."

Kay held Roselle out in front of her and smiled through moist eyes. "Welcome to our family, Roselle."

"Congratulations on your first guide dog puppy." Holly handed Kay the bag she had received on delivery day. "Thursday's Sightseer's meeting is at the mall, where we're taking a walk. I'm glad that I'll still get to see Roselle at meetings."

Holly followed Kay and Ted into the house and unclipped Roselle's leash. Roselle took in the living room, quietly exploring the couch and other furniture. *It is a nice house, but it isn't Holly's.*

"Roselle isn't usually this quiet," Holly said. "I think she is feeling shy. When she settles in, you'll discover that she is very playful and friendly, and as you can see, extremely sweet. She learns quickly too."

Roselle made her way down the hallway and through an open door, where she found a big bed and something under a chair that looked interesting. There were two of them exactly alike. She sniffed. *They're so fuzzy, and they smell like the lady named Kay.* Roselle wagged her tail harder and picked up one of the fuzzy things.

"Oh, my slippers!" Kay laughed. When she lifted Roselle up, the slipper was still hanging from her mouth. "Silly girl. I guess I need to find a better place for those."

"Leave it," Holly said firmly but with a hint of laughter in her voice.

Roselle loosed her jaw and let the slipper drop.

"See, I told you she's quick."

Kay hugged Roselle tight. "I'm in love already."

Me, too.

4

THE TERROR OF
THE NEIGHBORHOOD

Mike, 1956

Mike sat with three other students at his classroom table. He listened carefully as his teacher explained the assignment. She wanted them to draw a tree. *I know what a tree sounds like.*

Mike heard the scuffle of shoes and voices and tables scraping against the floor. At art time Mrs. Barton let them move their tables together so students could work with their friends, so Mike helped move his, too.

A year had passed since that exciting day when his kindergarten teacher in Chicago rested his fingers on that amazing letter "A" dot. Since then he'd learned all of his Braille letters and numbers. He'd learned to read some words and use the wonderful Braillewriter. Then Mike's father got a new job at a military installation called Plant 42 and the family moved from Chicago, Illinois, to Palmdale, California. In Palmdale everything was dry. "High desert," Dad called it. It didn't snow in winter and his new school did not have a special class for blind children. On top of that, because Chicago schools started kindergarten at age four and California schools started at five, Mike had to repeat kindergarten.

Mom and Dad had pushed hard to have Mike placed in a regular class at Yucca Elementary School, once again ignoring suggestions that Mike go away to an institution. Being in a regular class meant learning with the other children his age, but it also meant being the only blind child, and with no Braille to read or write.

Mike heard the gentle swish of a piece of paper being placed in front of him. "Here's your art paper, Mike."

"Thank you." From across the circle of desks, Mike could smell those mysterious wax sticks called crayons. Apparently, each one was a different color. Color seemed to be a big deal to people who could see.

"Your classmates will help you," Mrs. Barton assured him. "Won't you, children?"

The half-hearted "Yes, Mrs. Barton" told Mike what

he already knew—that they only said "yes" because "no" would get them sent to the corner.

Around him, crayons rubbed against paper over wooden desks. Mike felt for the box of crayons that the children shared and wrapped his fingers around one. Maybe he should draw an oak tree. Oak trees were tall and fat and dropped acorns. He touched the tip against the paper, feeling with his other hand to make sure he wasn't about to draw on the desk instead. He imagined the feeling of a tree trunk, hard and prickle-bumpy, and the smell like earth and leaves mixed. Oak leaves were small, sometimes soft and sometimes crunchy, depending on if it was spring or fall. Acorns were hard and shaped like little eggs with a pointy end. But how could he draw those? What color had he taken out of the box? He'd heard that leaves were green and bark was brown. *Do I have one of those?* His stomach tightened.

Mike ran his fingers over the smooth paper. He missed his cousins and Aunt Shirley. He missed running to the candy store and never being treated like a pain.

He cleared his throat. "Judy, can you help me draw a tree?"

"Not now, Mike," Judy said without lifting her head. "I'm concentrating."

He held out his crayon. "Roger, can you tell me what color this is?"

Roger didn't answer.

"It's blue," Mary said.

He put it back in the box and felt for another. Maybe this was tree-bark brown. He sniffed it, but it smelled exactly like the one that had been blue.

"What about this?"

Silence, except for a sigh from Judy.

He picked up his paper and held it out. "Can one of you just tell me where on the paper I should start the trunk?" Maybe it didn't matter what color he used. He could say he was being creative.

Suddenly someone snatched the paper out of Mike's hand so fast that it almost gave him a paper cut.

"Leave us alone," Roger snapped.

"Yeah," Judy said.

Roger crumpled Mike's paper and tossed it to the floor. Mike heard it land with a light tap, but the classroom was so quiet that it sounded more like a crash. He sat there, refusing to cry, feeling thirty pairs of eyes on him and that was never a good thing. He gripped the crayon in his hand so tightly that it snapped. He waited for Mrs. Barton to come over to see what was going on, but she stayed at her desk. Slowly, he returned the broken crayon to the box and reached for the crumpled ball that he'd felt hit his left foot. For the rest of art time, he sat, surrounded by the dull scratch of crayons and the smell of wax.

He did a lot of sitting and waiting at school while the rest of the class learned to add two plus two, read aloud, and do art projects. Moving to a new town and going to a different school had introduced Mike to something he'd never experienced before; for the first time ever, he felt alone and different. He listened to the teacher's lessons and did as much as he could in his head, but mostly he waited for parts of the day that didn't require sight to fully learn or appreciate, like story time and recess. At recess, he listened to the clink of rings and the shouts of boys and girls racing each other to the monkey bars, but he usually ended up playing alone once the kids realized that he couldn't see to catch a ball. The loneliness left him anxious to go home where he never heard "just sit and wait" while the rest of the family did something exciting or while Dad taught Ellery about how a radio worked or fixed something that involved a lot of great tools. His electrical mishap with the television had triggered an interest in anything electronic or scientific, and Mike's parents supported it 100 percent. Dad had just started teaching Mike a wonderful math game called algebra. He could already do it in his head.

X plus three equals 10. What is x?

Subtract three from 10, which equals seven. So x equals seven.

He started entertaining himself with algebra equations during art time.

♥ 🐈 ♥ 🐈 ♥

After the "sit-and-wait" school year, summer finally returned. Mike couldn't wait to spend his days playing with Ellery.

That was the summer Cindy moved to the neighborhood.

"Hi, Mike," Cindy called to him one day as she whizzed down the street on her bike.

"Hi, Cindy." Mike followed the hum of her tires. If he hadn't outgrown his pedal car, he could race her. He missed that car, and the freedom of flying around the living room, even if pedal cars were for little kids.

Cindy stopped her bike with a quick scratch-squeak.

"Neat bike." Mike reached out to stroke the handlebars. Plastic streamers hung from each handle. Girls. His bike would never have streamers. "Can I try it out?"

"Sure."

Cindy got off her bike and Mike moved in to take her place.

Cindy tugged on one of his feet, directing him to a pedal.

"I know where the pedals are," Mike informed her.

Ellery had a bike and Mike knew every inch of it. He moved his feet until the sides of his legs hit the pedals.

"Well, if you need to stop, push your foot back. Be sure to watch out for cars and other bikes and . . . Hang on one sec." Mike heard the slap of Cindy's sneakers then the scrape of a garbage can against cement. "Okay," Cindy shouted. "Now, keep the bike steady, push the pedals around, and go."

Mike gripped the handlebars and placed one foot on each pedal, pushing on the right pedal then the left. The bike wobbled to the right, but thanks to his quick right foot, he straightened it back out again. On his next try, his feet went around twice without a wobble.

"You're doing it," Cindy squealed.

Then he hit a bump and his feet weren't fast enough. Before he knew it, his elbow hit the pavement and Cindy was pulling the bike off him.

"Are you okay? Maybe I should've held it and walked beside you. That's what my dad did when he taught me to ride."

"No, I'm okay." Mike covered the hot stinging scrape on his elbow.

"You should clean that off."

Mike hopped up, brushing dirt off his pants. One knee was ripped, but only a little. "Can I have another chance when I get back?"

"Of course. You'll never learn if you don't keep trying."

Mike rushed inside. "Mom, I think I need a bandage!"

The click of metal told Mike that his mom was knitting something. If she were crocheting, he would only hear the light brush of the soft yarn against her fingers.

"What happened?"

"I tried Cindy's bike and fell off."

She set aside her knitting and directed Mike to the bathroom. "Be more careful next time, okay? The bike doesn't belong to you."

"I will."

Mrs. Hingson barely got the bandage on before Mike took off again. Cindy was waiting in the driveway. Just as with the pedal car, neither parent reacted as if blindness should stop him from an activity that any other boy his age enjoyed.

By the end of the week, Mike could ride all the way down the block without falling. With the help of his echolocation, he dodged cars, trashcans, and his neighborhood friends. Ellery and the other kids thought nothing of seeing Mike zoom around on Cindy's bike.

Cindy's bike became Mike's ticket to freedom until Dad finally decided, "I think it's time for you to have your own bike."

As soon as Dad got the bike home, Ellery challenged Mike, "Race you!"

It didn't matter to Mike that the bike had been used before or that it was only a 20-incher, because it was all his! Off they rode, exploring the streets of Palmdale until dinnertime. But the family quickly learned that not everyone was impressed by the sight of the reddish-blond-haired eight-year-old, who couldn't see, on wheels.

One afternoon, Mike came in hot and sweaty from riding. He tried not to slam the screen door in his rush for a glass of water.

"Shh." Mom touched Mike's shoulder. "Your father is on the phone."

Mike quietly opened the cupboard where Mom kept glasses.

"Well," Dad said, "he was just out riding his bike." There was an edge in Dad's voice.

Mike stood back. Had he done something wrong without meaning to?

"Yes, I'm aware that Mike is the blind one."

Mom sighed. Mike groaned. This, again?

Pause.

"Did he crash into anything?"

Another pause. Mike turned the water on low to get a drink. He felt the coldness rise through the glass until it almost reached the rim, then turned off the faucet.

Dad let out a long, slow breath. "Then what's the problem?"

After another pause, Dad set the receiver down. Hard.

Mom was finally free to vent her frustration. "Another one of those calls? This is getting ridiculous."

"Yep. I don't know what offends the neighbors more: the idea of a blind child riding a bike or the fact that we allow it."

"'Do you know what your son is doing?'" Mom imitated a female neighbor. "As if we don't keep track of our boys. Or Mike is vandalizing someone's home."

"Or you don't know which of your kids is blind," Mike added.

Ellery came in with a slam. "What did I miss?"

"The terror of the neighborhood strikes again," Dad muttered on his way back to the garage.

Mike's parents got a lot of calls from neighbors. Mike couldn't figure out why they were so upset. No one called to report Ellery riding his bike. Mike was in Boy Scouts, children's choir at church, and had even started piano lessons. Why did people worry about him riding his bike?

Good thing they didn't know about all the times that Mr. Judd, the mailman, let him drive the mail truck.

But the family refused to let the criticism bother

them. Mike and Ellery lived on their bikes that summer. And when the new school year started, Mike rode his bike to school with his brother and all the other kids.

He still did more sitting and waiting at school than reading and writing, but home provided a refuge where he was treated as perfectly normal.

Before Mike knew it, Christmas had come.

On Christmas morning, Mike unwrapped a gift that the neighbors definitely wouldn't approve of.

"Is this what I think it is?" Mike ran his hands over the box, wishing it was marked with Braille so he could find out more quickly. But when he shook the box it sounded exactly like what he'd been asking for—a kit for building a radio. This radio consisted of a board with wires to string across and attach to a battery.

"It is indeed." Dad sounded almost as excited as Mike was. "We can put it together this week while you're out of school. Just let me read the instructions so I can help you along."

"Can I connect all the wires?"

"I wouldn't have it any other way."

Mike soon discovered that his new kit allowed him to build 10 different kinds of simple radio receivers and transmitters. It wasn't long before he learned about every part in the kit and could assemble all 10 radio sets from memory. He spent hours with his new present and even came up with a few original designs on his own.

Now Mike had a new activity to think about and plan while sitting at his desk during art time.

5

ROSELLE ON THE TOWN

Roselle, 1998

"Roselle, come!" Kay Stern called from her bedroom. Roselle crouched down and scooted under the coffee table, the slipper still in her mouth. Kay had left her closet door open just enough for Roselle to get to the slipper. *I wonder why humans are such slow learners.*

"Ted," Kay called, "can you get Roselle's stuff together please? We're running late already and I think she just declared a game of Hide and Seek."

Roselle saw Kay's legs from under the coffee table.

"Roselle, come."

This time Roselle slid out from under the table and ran to Kay. She stopped and stood obediently at her raiser's feet, the slipper dangling.

"Roselle, you little sneak. Give me my slipper."

She reached for it. Roselle raced to hide behind a chair.

"Oh, so we're combining Keep Away, Steal the Slipper, and Hide and Seek this time. You are getting very clever, Roselle."

Stealing Kay's slippers never stopped being fun. Kay looked especially funny when searching for them while in a big hurry to clean up for company. She scurried around, searching under tables and behind furniture. *Apparently, humans don't enjoy having slippers lying around for their friends to see. That seems silly. Slippers are cool.*

Kay leapt around the side of the chair before Roselle could escape. "Leave it."

Roselle wagged her tail, but the look on Kay's face told her the game was over. She dropped the slipper. Kay swooped down and retrieved it. "Good thing you don't have a habit of hiding my car keys. I'd be in real trouble then." Roselle detected a slight grin on Kay's face as she pointed a finger. "And don't you get any ideas."

Roselle just stared. *Why would I want to steal keys? They aren't fuzzy or soft, and the jingle would give me away every time.*

In the past few months, Roselle had grown from about 15 pounds to 50 and traded a roly-poly puppy body for a tall, long-legged frame that reached above Kay's knees, but she was still very much a puppy.

Since moving in with the Sterns, she'd grown accustomed to going everywhere with her puppy raisers. She went to church, to the grocery store, on trips to visit family, even to concerts at the music academy. The goal was to expose her to as much as possible so she could feel comfortable and learn to be calm in any situation.

On Thursday evenings they attended Sightseers meetings, where they got to see Holly. Sometimes they met in a public place like a park; other times they met at the home of Marcia and Phil, the club leaders. Puppy raisers talked about their progress and helped those experiencing problems. Some of the raisers shared funny stories; others cried because they missed a dog that they just sent back to the Guide Dogs campus. All the dogs sat at their raisers' feet, watching each other, waiting for the moment when they could play together. Some people called this playtime recess, but the dogs just called it fun. Today was Saturday, when they went to Solvang. A man named Jack Brey led those meetings, where members talked about club business and new training techniques.

Kay returned the slipper to her bedroom. Roselle entertained herself with a Nylabone until the Sterns called her to the door, Kay holding the puppy coat and Ted the leash and the Gentle Leader. I love my coat. Putting the coat on means something fun is about the happen. Too bad other dogs don't have it this good.

Sometimes when they took walks, Roselle would see a dog wearing a horrible thing called a choke chain collar. If the dog pulled on the leash, spikes poked his throat. She felt sad for those dogs, especially when their owners yanked them hard and yelled, "No," or "Knock it off," or the worst: "Dumb dog!" The Gentle Leader worked just like it sounded: a soft strap wrapped around Roselle's head and muzzle like a halter on a horse. If she pulled her leash, those straps reminded her to stop. They also helped guide her in the direction that the Sterns wanted her to go.

Ted and Kay never spoke harshly when Roselle made a mistake or got distracted by something like a car horn or kids throwing one of those wonderful-looking toys called a ball that guide dog puppies weren't allowed to have.

When this happened, Kay or Ted corrected her just firmly enough so Roselle knew they meant it and gave her Gentle Leader a tug in the right direction. When she obeyed a command, they stroked her head, smiled, and said, "Good girl." Guide dog raisers were taught to encourage obedience with lots of praise. Roselle and other puppies-in-training knew that "Leave it" never brought the strokes and smiles that "Good girl" did, so they wanted to obey. Too bad the owners of those poor dogs with the choke collars didn't understand.

Dressed in her coat and wearing the Gentle Leader, Roselle followed the Sterns to the car, this time led by Ted. As always, Roselle walked on the left side of her person.

Holly was the first to greet them at the Solvang meeting. Holly had a new puppy in her arms. Roselle fought the urge to make friends without permission. Being distracted by other dogs was one area where Roselle struggled. That, and eating food that wasn't in her special dish. She looked up at the puppy. The puppy looked down at Roselle and whimpered. Roselle almost let out a friendly bark to say, "It's okay, you don't need to be afraid," but she managed to keep quiet. Instead she gave the puppy her most friendly doggy smile.

"Good girl, Roselle," Kay said. "What an improvement!"

"Yes." Holly stroked her puppy. "You're learning, Roselle. I'll bet that next week, you won't even notice him."

I will notice him. I notice everything. But I'll be cool about it.

♥ 🐾 ♥ 🐾 ♥

The next morning they went to church. When Kay said, "Roselle, down," she found her favorite spot on the floor between Ted and Kay's feet and rested her head in her paws as the music began. Time for a nap. Ted and Kay's friends joked that Roselle slept through church because she was bored by the minister's sermon, but honestly, she was just tired. Practicing commands like "Roselle, come," attending puppy club meetings, focusing so hard, and playing all those games of Hide and Seek took a lot out of a dog. Sure, her life wasn't all work. When the coat came off at home, she could play and run like other dogs, but she did very little lying around.

She awoke to the sound of the Sterns and their friends laughing.

"She's snoring again."

"From the look on the minister's face, I think he's starting to take it personally."

Roselle looked up and yawned. *What are they talking about? I don't snore.*

It was a good thing she took that nap because on the way home, they went out to lunch and ran errands.

Roselle followed Kay's direction through an automatic door into a place that she'd come to know as the grocery store. She stood back as Ted got a shopping cart. Roselle walked at Kay's left, trying not to let the smiles of shoppers pull her away. People are so nice and fun to watch. They seemed to like her and she wanted to like every one of them back, but she needed to focus.

Ted stopped the cart in front of a cold wall of shelves. Even through the plastic packaging, Roselle smelled it—meat. She lifted her nose for a whiff, stepping forward just a little. Then she saw Kay's face looking unhappy and stepped back.

Kay praised her. A lady pushing a shopping cart grinned at Roselle as if she understood how hard it had been to leave that beef and chicken.

At the same store just a few weeks before, Roselle had obeyed Kay's instruction to leave a mountain of bananas only to be tempted by some carrots. The man in charge of the produce department gave them a look that said he wasn't pleased to have a dog in the store, particularly a dog that licked his carrots, so Kay took Roselle outside and let Ted finish the shopping. Later, they returned to apologize, and the manager agreed to give Roselle another chance. Maybe he let her come back because, as Kay and Ted said, she was becoming popular around town. *Whatever popular means, it sounds good and I don't want to mess it up.*

Roselle worked hard to keep her head up as they shopped each aisle, even though everything in her wanted to walk nose to the ground like other dogs. It is crucial for guide dogs to look ahead, watch for obstacles, and listen and smell for anything a blind person couldn't see. Roselle was also learning to feel for obstacles and movement through her paws, fur, whiskers, and body vibrations.

"So, how is my favorite customer?" The cashier peered over the check-out stand as Ted and Kay transferred their groceries from the cart to the counter.

"Roselle is doing great." Kay set a bag of apples down. "We took her to a play the other night and she made it through the entire performance. There was even gunfire on stage. She looked up like, 'What's that?' Then she decided, 'Oh well, nothing I guess,' and lay back down. Next week she is participating in the Fourth of July Parade."

"She'll be a hit, I'm sure."

There was only one problem with events like parades: the food. Roselle would be bombarded by falling popcorn, spilled soda, and children tossing unwanted hot dogs her way.

Leaving such things was hard enough at home.

Every time it happened, she promised herself it would never happen again. She knew the rules: food and water from her dishes only and only when Ted or Kay said, "Okay." Then a shred of cheese would fly off Kay's grater and sail down past her nose smelling so delicious, and she would snatch up the creamy fleck before Kay could say, "Leave it."

Once she saw a dog eat a grasshopper at the park, so when she spotted one in the backyard, she licked it up when Kay wasn't looking. It tasted bitter and its legs kicked around in her mouth. "Leave it" was easy that time. *Yuck.*

Kay and Ted had started tempting Roselle with food, forcing her to practice leaving it alone. The day before Fourth of July, Kay placed a chunk of leftover cooked hamburger on the kitchen floor and stood back. Roselle's mouth watered. *Smells so good.* She'd taken some before, so she knew it also tasted good. *Really good. And juicy.*

This is just mean. She looked up at Kay, then down at the meat.

Kay pretended to read a magazine.

Roselle licked her lips. She let out a long breath. The scent of the meat reminded her of a barbecue, another thing that humans got to enjoy while she lay under the picnic table and waited until it was time for her perfectly measured but boring kibble.

Before temptation could win, Roselle turned and walked away from the meat.

"Good girl!" Kay called to her.

Roselle comforted herself with her Nylabone. *Sometimes being a good girl stinks.* Other dogs got to eat off the floor. They even got treats. She saw it happen at the park and on TV all the time. *Why not me? I work so much harder than they do.* But as Jack Brey and the other Sightseers constantly reminded puppy raisers, she needed to learn to do her job, and part of that included staying away from food that didn't belong to her so she could be trusted in restaurants, cafeterias, stores, and kitchens.

The parade, with all the music and people, made the frustration worth it. Many of her friends from Sightseers were there.

Summer ended and Roselle got to be part of another fun event called Montecito Beautification Day. Then came Christmas and Roselle learned to leave the toys on the big, lighted tree alone.

At one Sightseers meeting, Roselle heard Ted and Kay talking to Holly.

"We've decided to take Roselle to New York. We have an apartment there. We figure it'll be a good experience for her to learn to deal with the crowds, riding the subway, and other parts of city life. And she'll get to fly in an airplane for the first time."

New York? Airplane? That sounds like fun!

6

DOG WITH A JOB

Mike, 1959

Mike followed Ellery and his parents into the house. Rudy, the family's dachshund, ran down the hall to greet him.

"Hey, girl." Mike rubbed the small black dog's back, his mind more on his plans than on his dog.

"Change out of your church clothes, boys." Mom sounded rushed. "We're having guests for lunch, remember?"

If he changed quickly, maybe he could get started on his new radio project before lunch. While he worked, he would listen to the book that arrived in the mail on Friday.

A year before, Mr. and Mrs. Hingson had found out about a program called Talking Books, which provided recorded books for the blind free of charge. The "books" arrived as a box of vinyl records—round black discs with a Braille label in the center of each one. They also provided a special record player. Most stories required several records. As soon as Mike finished one book, he mailed it back in the return box, and Talking Books sent the next title on Mike's list. Most of the books were older, and it took a long time for new titles to be recorded and become available, but Mike didn't care. The stories were new to him. At nine years old, he loved books of any kind.

This time, they had sent a book called *The Mixed-Up Twins*. The title alone sounded intriguing. Were they mixed up as in confused, or did people get them mixed up because they were twins? He couldn't wait to find out.

"Mike, clean your room before lunch."

Mike's arms dropped with the weight of disappointment. *What about electronics and The Mixed-Up Twins?*

"Don't worry, you can listen to your story while you work."

"Okay." Mike started unfastening his tie.

That was one nice thing about recorded books; a kid could listen anytime, even while doing chores.

The previous week, Dad had been reading the Sunday paper when he saw an article about a new teacher in town. Edwards Air Force Base had hired her to teach the children of military workers.

"Her name is Sharon Gold and she is blind." Dad showed Mom, Ellery, and Mike the article, which also talked about her German shepherd, Nola, who went everywhere with her, including her classroom. Nola was no ordinary dog; she was a guide dog, trained especially for blind people.

From the moment Dad read the article, Mike had been fascinated by Sharon and Nola, so today she was coming over for Sunday dinner. Other than the children in his kindergarten class in Chicago, Mike didn't know any other blind people. He had never met a blind adult and was amazed by the idea of a guide dog. Curiosity pushed *The Mixed-Up Twins* to the back of his mind. He rushed around, running his hands over his bedroom floor picking up toys and the dirty socks that he forgot to put in the hamper while getting ready for church in the morning. If Sharon was anything like him, lack of eyesight would not prevent her from noticing a messy room. In fact, she would probably be the first to detect the odor of dirty socks.

The anticipation of meeting Sharon distracted Mike for the rest of the morning, even as he practiced piano.

"C sharp, Mike, not D sharp," Mom called from the kitchen.

He blamed it on the Braille music, but deep down

he knew he was just lost in his thoughts. He'd memorized the notes days ago so he wouldn't have to rely on reading the Braille sheets. *I wonder if Sharon plays piano?*

Finally, two hours later, with the smell of Mom's pot roast wafting from the kitchen, Sharon and her roommate Cheryl arrived. Rudy let out a growl-bark before Nola even entered.

"Mike. Ellery," Dad rested his hand on Mike's shoulder. "This is Sharon."

"Nice to meet you, boys." Sharon's voice was friendly, like she smiled a lot. "I'm sure you've heard about Nola."

Rudy sniffed Nola, but Nola didn't bark or growl. "Sharon, why don't you explain Nola's job?"

"Well, Nola is trained to watch and listen for the things I can't see, like steps, curbs, fire hydrants, and moving cars. Come over here so you can feel her harness, Mike."

Mike and his brother walked over to Sharon, and she set Mike's hand on a short bar connected to two longer bars that were attached to a special collar around Nola's head.

"This harness helps me direct Nola and feel which way she is guiding me. So really, we're a team."

"She's cool," Ellery said.

Mike let go of the harness and ran his hands over Nola's thick fur.

"Let me take off her harness so you can pet her. I'm not supposed to let you when it's on. After lunch, you can take her outside if you'd like."

"Can I?" Mike asked his parents.

"Sure, since Sharon offered."

After they sat down to eat and Dad said grace, Mike and Ellery bombarded Sharon with questions. They learned that Sharon taught elementary school. The fact that Sharon worked perked Mike's interest. He'd heard that a lot of blind adults stayed home and let other people take care of them, with their only income coming from the government. Many of them felt sorry for themselves for being blind, which never made sense to him. Sharon acted no different than her roommate Cheryl or any of his parents' friends from the neighborhood or church. She had hobbies and didn't seem to feel bad about being blind at all. She obviously understood, like Mike and his family, that being blind wasn't the end of the world. It just meant you had to do things a little differently.

"Can I take Nola out to the backyard now?" Mike asked after lunch.

"Go ahead." Sharon handed Nola's leash over to Mike.

Nola walked calmly on Mike's left side as they headed through the kitchen out into the yard. Mike sat down on the grass to pet Nola. He ran his fingertips up her pointed ears and down her long muzzle and cold, wet nose. Nola sniffed him all over. Mike laughed. He grabbed her collar and prepared to stand up, but suddenly, Nola stiffened, like she saw something on the other side of the yard. She jumped up and ran, dragging Mike across the grass.

"Nola, what are you doing?" Mike hollered, sliding on his stomach, his hand still clutching Nola's leash. What had happened to the calm dog he'd been petting just a few minutes before? He tried to stop himself with his hands, but it was no use. Nola was too strong.

Just when Mike thought he might collide with the fence or a tree, Nola stopped. Her wagging tail whipped against Mike's arms.

"Did you see a bird or something?" Mike caught his breath. He hopped up and wiped damp grass and dirt off the back of his jeans. Mom was going to be mad.

Nola just wagged her tail more, panting heavily. Mike heard a smile under her breath. She clearly loved this game.

"Wow, Nola. I've never been dragged by a dog before." Mike started laughing again. He'd never had this much fun with a dog before, either.

He ran back to the house with Nola to tell the grownups about his adventure. Sharon and her friend cracked up.

"I forgot to warn you. When the harness comes off, Nola is an ordinary German shepherd."

Sharon became a good friend to Mike and his family after that day. He quickly learned how to handle her energetic 100-pound dog. Knowing Sharon showed him something else too; he now knew he wasn't alone. There were other blind people in Palmdale. Better yet, he knew a blind woman who was out in her community making a difference. He'd been in school long enough to know that teaching wasn't an easy job. If she can do it, I can do it, Mike decided. Maybe he wouldn't become a teacher, but he would do something. And he definitely hoped to have a dog like hers. Nola seemed like she was a friend to Sharon in addition to being a guide. *A best friend. I'm still waiting to find one of those.* A dog would be so much more fun than a white cane, something he had never used but knew most blind people relied on. You couldn't slide across the backyard with a cane or talk to it or play games with it.

The more Sharon visited, the more Mike noticed how she and Nola seemed to read each other's minds. What would it be like to have someone know what he needed without him having to say anything? At the same time, he also understood that Sharon didn't seem so dependent on the dog that she was helpless without her. That must have been what she meant about them being a team, and that seemed really cool. Friends should be a team, he thought.

"Can anyone get a guide dog?" Mike asked one evening, feeling Nola's tail brush against his leg as he finished his dessert.

Sharon swallowed a bite. "Well, you have to apply, and the minimum age is 16. Mr. and Mrs. Hingson, you should consider applying when Mike is old enough."

Sharon told the family about the Guide Dogs for the Blind campus in San Rafael, where blind people trained for four weeks before going home with a dog. "You have a few years, but it would give Mike a lot of freedom when the time comes."

Waiting until I'm 16? Feels like forever.

"We're already starting to think ahead to when Mike goes to Palmdale High School," Dad said. "It's a large, complicated campus, nothing like elementary school where everything is easy to find."

Mike had learned to use his echolocation to hear the support columns of the covered walkways and other landmarks that helped him get around school without help, but high school sounded a little scary. He imagined himself arriving on the first day of high school accompanied by a large German shepherd. No one would dare mess with him, and being the only kid with a dog at school might make him very popular. *I'll never sit alone again.*

Over the next summer, Mike set aside thoughts of a dog and took another big step when he and his mom studied Braille. Mike hadn't used the skill since kindergarten in Chicago. His parents had worked with the school district in Palmdale to arrange for Braille instruction. Since Mike had learned it earlier in his life, Mom thought they could get a head start by studying reading and writing in Braille over the summer. He and his parents went to the Braille Institute of America in Los Angeles in late June to get some instruction books. The Braille Institute was also the place where Mike got his Talking Books, so it was doubly fun to go there since he could get new records to listen to. His parents ordered a Braillewriter from Germany and Mike got right to work, hoping to be able to read and write by September.

By the time Mike started fourth grade, there were other blind students in Palmdale. He transferred to a new school across town called Tamarisk, which served fourth through sixth graders from all over the district. He met Mrs. Hershberger, who worked with blind students so they could have Braille books and other equipment that they needed while also being assigned to regular classrooms. Going to Tamarisk meant he could no longer ride his bike to school with Ellery and the other neighborhood kids. Instead, he had to take the bus and experience loneliness all over again as he adjusted to a new school.

For the first time, Mike had schoolbooks printed in Braille so he could read along during every subject instead of just listening. There was only one problem with Braille books—they were much bigger than ordinary books. Far fewer Braille words fit on a page than printed words, and Braille required thick paper, similar to plastic. In fifth grade, Mrs. Hershberger decided that the ordinary wooden desks with the lift-up top that the other kids used simply wouldn't do for Mike. He needed something larger to hold those books.

Months later, a special desk was delivered to Mike's classroom.

"Look at that," one of his classmates said as Mike started checking it out.

"That's a neat desk, Mike."

Mike ran his hands over the top and sides. The wooden desk was shaped like a number seven, with a corkboard top that wrapped around. It had two book-and-storage shelves along the right side and an open compartment right under the desktop. The cork kept papers from sliding around as Mike read with his fingers.

"This can hold everything!" Mike started arranging his books on the shelves as a few curious students watched.

That desk traveled with Mike to sixth grade, on to

junior high, and even to high school, but for today he savored the rare moments of being the center of attention at school for having something no one else had.

7

GOODBYE, SANTA BARBARA

Roselle, 1999

"Taxi!" Ted waved his arm.

Cars whizzed past on the busy Manhattan Street. Tall buildings towered over Roselle. The white stuff that Ted and Kay called "snow" chilled her paws. I like the way it looks and smells, so fluffy and clean. Sometimes flakes fell on her tongue. They melted into wet drops before she could decide what they tasted like. Squatting over it to do her business on the other hand? That, she didn't like at all. It seemed like it took hours for her tail and the backs of her legs to dry off and warm up. It was worse than when she had to do it at the airport with all those people around. How humiliating.

"You are being such a trooper with the snow and

slushy streets," Kay told her as they stepped away from an icy patch.

One taxi zoomed by without stopping. A second one slowed down and started pulling up to the curb.

"Finally," Kay whispered. But before Ted could open the back door, the cab driver sped off again.

"What is wrong?" Ted smacked his leg. "We had the same problem yesterday."

Roselle could feel his frustration. Around them, people rushed and shoved. Why are people so pushy in New York? No one stopped to smile at her or ask, "So, how is my favorite tourist?"

Since arriving in New York, they'd attended a play, gone to museums, walked in Central Park, and shopped in big stores. But now that they needed to "hail a cab" as Ted called it, no one would stop.

"The problem is," Kay said, "we have a dog with us and coat or no coat, she isn't an official service dog yet, so they aren't bound by the same laws."

Ted looked at Roselle. Roselle stood still, looking back up at him. *I'm the problem?* She cocked her head to one side. *I'm sorry.*

"I guess we can take the subway again." Kay slipped her coat sleeve up to check her watch. "But we might be late for the concert."

"No, wait." Ted rested a hand on Kay's arm just as Roselle spotted another cab heading in their direction. The vibration on the street tickled her paws. "Stand behind me, far enough so we don't look like we're together."

Kay and Roselle obeyed. Kay smirked like she knew what her husband was up to.

The cab pulled up.

"Thanks," Ted hopped in the back but didn't close the door. While telling the driver where they wanted to go, he waved his arm and scooted over. Kay and Roselle hopped over the muddy gutter and onto the backseat. Roselle hurried to her spot on the floor. Kay shut the door. They were in!

The driver gazed into the rearview mirror and spotted Roselle.

Kay leaned forward. "Before you get upset, let me assure you that this dog is trained to be still and obedient and will not leave an unwanted gift in your cab. We are required to keep her updated on shots and squeaky clean, so she does not have fleas or any other vermin for you to worry about."

He still looked hesitant.

"Hey, we went to a Broadway show last night and they let her in."

"Okay, but if that dog leaves a mess or chews the seat, I'm sending you the bill."

"Agreed."

If Roselle could get through the five-and-a-half-hour airplane ride without causing a problem, she could certainly handle a short taxi trip. She'd spent most of the flight curled in a ball between Kay and Ted's feet. Now that she was full-grown—about 20 inches high and almost 60 pounds—it was getting harder to squeeze into small places. Taking off felt strange, and once in a while the plane started to shake. But when Roselle looked up at Ted and Kay, they seemed relaxed and reassured her, "It's okay," so she went back to sleep until they landed. Plane travel is a breeze.

The taxi trip ended before Roselle could even curl up.

"Thank you so much," Kay said as they got out.

They headed for the concert hall. Roselle slept through the concert of classical music just as she did when they attended performances at the music academy at home. All of the education she had received from her puppy raisers was paying off.

Kay praised her as they left the concert hall. "You're becoming a real pro. It's hard to believe that we will be returning to California soon, and then it won't be long before your real training begins."

Time went quickly after that exciting trip. New puppies joined Sightseers and grown ones left for campus. Some left only to return, after being dropped from the program or career changed. Changing careers meant the dog got to serve humans in a different way, like becoming a therapy dog, learning to detect seizures, or even learning to warn a diabetic person when their blood sugar was too high or low. Dogs could be dropped for all kinds of reasons such as health problems, ear infections, less-than-perfect hearing, or a tendency to disobey or be too nervous. Some even got dropped for stopping to relieve themselves too often while in harness, which all puppies-in-training knew was a big no-no. If a dog got dropped, his or her puppy raisers got first dibs on adoption. Some raisers even got the chance to adopt their former puppies after they were retired. Roselle noticed that Sightseer members were very proud of the dogs they had raised and loved to give updates.

"The dog I raised last year was just assigned to a blind college student."

"Otto got career changed and was adopted by a family with a blind child who was too young for a guide dog."

"Brit is developing arthritis and needs to be retired. Her handler can't keep her, so guess who is coming home to live with us?"

During one Sightseers meeting at the park, Roselle noticed that Kay looked sad. She nudged her raiser's knee. Kay rested her hand on Roselle's head, rubbing gently with her fingers. With her other hand she dabbed at her eyes. What was wrong?

"Everyone," Marcia announced, "This is Roselle's

last week with us."

It is?

"Yeah." Kay looked down at Roselle. "We are driving her back to San Rafael this weekend."

"The year certainly flew by." Ted patted his wife's hand.

"Well, she is definitely ready." Holly wrapped her arm around Kay. "But I bet you aren't."

Ted let out a laugh, "I think the only one who won't miss Roselle is our pastor."

The week passed quickly. On Friday, Kay and Ted packed the car and called Roselle. She wasn't far away since she had taken to supervising the packing process to make sure her toys and other stuff made it into the bag. Something feels different. Roselle could sense it in the air and in the sadness coming from her raisers. Kay and Ted were quiet and Kay kept stepping away from the suitcase to wipe away tears. Roselle nuzzled Kay's hand to tell her everything would be okay. Just before everyone climbed into the car, Kay gave Roselle a big hug.

"Roselle," she said, "we are so sad to see you go, but you have a job to do. It's time for our life together to end. You be a good girl and learn to be the best guide dog there is, okay? You can do it, I know it."

She didn't like the sound of "see you go." Hopping into the car felt like taking a ride to the vet. Roselle fought the desire to pace the backseat like she'd seen other nervous dogs do before stopping at the window to send a silent "help me" look to passing cars. She sat still like she'd been trained to do and released her anxiety through heavy panting.

The trip to campus took about six hours. The car grew quieter as Ted's car pulled off the freeway in San Rafael, late in the afternoon.

"You are in for a great adventure." Kay smiled at Roselle over the back of her seat. "You are going to meet lots of other dogs during training."

"You'd think it was her first day of kindergarten." Ted sounded just as melancholy as his wife.

"I feel more like I'm sending her off to college." Kay reached over the seat to pet Roselle. "I know you will make a wonderful guide, but if it doesn't work out or you decide you don't want to do it, you have a lifelong home with us."

"Speaking of college," Ted pointed toward a large building. "It looks sort of like one."

Kay grabbed a handful of tissues and stuffed them in her pocket as they pulled into the parking lot of the campus. Roselle peered out the window. The shade trees and sunny paths looked vaguely familiar but somehow smaller. She spotted a man with a young boy walking from the big building. The boy held an empty leash. His father draped his arm around the boy's shoulders.

"Well, here we go." Kay took a deep breath and

opened her door.

The quieter and sadder the Sterns got the more nervous Roselle felt. Now she knew for sure that this was not another fun outing.

Up the steps and through the glass door they went, until they reached a tall desk.

"We're Kay and Ted Stern," Kay said, "Here to drop off our angel."

Drop off. I don't like the sound of that either.

A black Lab lay beside the desk. He looked wise as he stared into Roselle's eyes. Was he one of the friends that Kay said she would meet?

"Feel free to walk around campus with Roselle and stay as long as you like," The lady behind the desk said after Kay checked in. She showed the three of them to a small room. "Just bring her back here when you're ready."

They stood there for a moment, no one knowing what to do or say.

"Would you like to take a tour?" The lady suggested.

"That would be wonderful."

She told the Sterns where the tours began and they joined a small group of families. They visited the puppy kennel where clusters of yellow, black, and golden pups pressed their noses to the wire, begging for attention. Most of the families in their tour group were also dropping off dogs, so a cloud of sadness hung over the tour, even as they approached the best part of campus.

"Roselle, look at that wonderful play area." Roselle watched a bunch of dogs romp and chase each other through tunnels like she once had as an eight-week-old puppy.

They visited the puppy training classrooms and met a few of the teachers. Kay and Ted laughed when the tour guide showed them what some called the Spa, where dogs were bathed and groomed.

"You are going to love it here," Kay told Roselle.

Roselle watched another yellow Lab march past with a man wearing a blindfold. It was beautiful place, and all the dogs and people seemed so nice. But she loved Ted and Kay, too. *Maybe I don't want to be a guide dog after all. How can I let Kay know that a lifelong home with her sounds just right?*

"We should probably get going," Ted whispered. "The longer we stay, the harder it'll be."

"I know." Kay bit her bottom lip as they headed for the main building and told the lady at the desk that they were ready to turn Roselle in.

They followed the lady down the hall to the private room she had shown them earlier. "Take as much time as you need," she said before shutting the door.

Ted patted Roselle's back. "You are a good dog, Roselle. I know you'll pass with flying colors."

Kay knelt beside Roselle, wiping away tears as

they trickled down her cheeks. Roselle wanted to lick them up and make her feel better, but licking wasn't allowed and she was feeling just as sad.

"Thank you for being such a precious part of our lives." Kay wrapped her arms around Roselle's neck. She took her face in her hands and kissed her head. "I am going to miss you so much, especially that crooked little smile of yours."

I'm going to miss you, too. So much. Roselle touched her nose to Kay's cheek, giving her a kiss in return.

Ted opened the door while Kay was still kneeling on the floor with Roselle. "We're ready," he said through a tight throat.

The lady walked in and squeezed Kay's arm as she took Roselle's leash. She reached into her pocket and pulled out a tissue for her. The handful in Kay's pocket had already been used up.

"I know this is a hard day. It doesn't matter how many puppies you raise. Turning them in always feels like losing a family member."

Kay nodded as Ted took her hand.

"See you at graduation, girl." Ted waved.

Roselle stopped for one more look at her puppy raisers before following the volunteer out the door and down the hall.

Through the glass door, Roselle spotted a parade of puppies out for their afternoon walk. They looked so little and funny with their tiny ears bouncing and their oversized paws. They looked . . . happy. Suddenly she felt happy, too.

8

A NEW KIND OF FREEDOM

Mike, 1964

Mike listened for the *whoosh, thud* of the newspaper hitting the porch of the house on Sumac Street. A year ago, Ellery had gotten a job delivering papers and asked Mike to share it with him. Thanks to a tandem bike built for two, they rode the route together, splitting the papers and the pay. Mike was now 14 and in the eighth grade, so he was always looking for ways to earn his own money. He was quickly growing out of his kid body into a lanky teenager.

The soles of Ellery's tennis shoes hit the ground with a dull *skritch.* Mike let his feet fall, too.

"Is he there?"

"Yep, he just grabbed the paper."

Mike heard the familiar creak of a front door,

followed by the jingle of the dog's collar. This customer on Sumac Street owned the smartest dog in Palmdale. Almost every time they delivered, the dog waited on the porch for Ellery and Mike to ride up with the paper. As soon as the rolled-up newspaper hit the porch, the dog hopped up and grabbed it, then dropped the paper by the door and pulled a tennis ball that hung from a string tied to the door handle. Once the door was open, he picked up the paper again, took it inside, and shut the door with his muzzle.

"Too bad we can't train Peewee to fetch our paper," Ellery said. After Rudy died the year before, the Hingsons had adopted Peewee, a miniature dachshund.

That house on Sumac Street was the highlight of Mike and Ellery's route. The rest of the morning went quickly and uneventfully, with Ellery tossing his papers and Mike tossing his knowing that some neighbors were most likely standing by expecting him to miss because he couldn't see the porch in front of him. But he knew exactly where each one was, so he rarely missed. Sharing his 16-year-old brother's paper route made Mike feel like an ordinary teenager. He seized every opportunity to tell a "while-I-was-delivering-papers" story since he didn't have a sport to brag about like other guys.

On school days they went straight from their early-morning route to getting ready for school, but on Sundays, the brothers read together until Mom and Dad got up for church. Ellery usually did the reading on Sundays. It would be a long time before their favorite James Bond and science fiction novels made it to Talking Books, and Mike didn't want to miss out on a single one.

Sometimes when Ellery didn't feel like reading, Mike went into Dad's den to play with the short wave radio receiver. He and Dad enjoyed listening to radio stations from around the world. Not only had they discovered music stations, but as his dad explained, there were many other signals that ham radio operators used just for talking to each other.

Dad learned that people could get a license from the government, allowing them to have a radio transmitter in the home. With the transmitter and a receiver, the person could not only listen but also talk with other radio operators. Mike couldn't wait to get his ham radio license, but first he needed to learn the required subjects, including knowing the signals that came across as tones called Morse code. In the meantime, while other kids his age talked on the phone or hung out, he listened to the licensed operators talking with each other, learned Morse code, and checked out every book on ham radio that Talking Books had available.

Mike was still active in Boy Scouts and earning

merit badges. By the time Mike had entered eighth grade, he had earned the rank of Star Scout, which meant that he had earned five merit badges. One of the first badges he earned was his Signaling badge, which meant that he had to demonstrate—among other things—that he understood Morse code. Earning the badges brought a great sense of accomplishment and feeling that he belonged and was doing what other guys his age enjoyed. The day finally came when he and Dad earned their ham radio license, giving him another major achievement to be proud of. At school, on the other hand, he continued to feel like an outsider.

Like every other eighth grade student, Mike had to take Physical Education (PE), but just as he had experienced in his first few years of elementary school, Mike couldn't always participate in the same activities as the other kids. While the rest of the students played basketball or another sport, Mike did an alternative activity such as jumping rope. He did get to join the class sometimes when they ran around the track, but most of the time, he was on his own. The teachers kept an eye on him but Mike knew he stood out. He could hear guys laughing, girls cheering each other on, the teacher's whistle, and the sounds made it all the more frustrating that he couldn't be part of it. He'd heard that junior high was a difficult time for everyone, that growing from a child to a teenager involved a lot of changes and confusion. But his classmates seemed to have something to help them through it all that he lacked. They had each other. PE was a constant reminder that he spent more time alone than most other 14-year-olds.

On one of these lonely spring school days, the class was playing baseball while Mike enjoyed the one sport he excelled at.

"Michael, you have a visitor," his PE teacher called out.

Mike stopped jumping as he heard a man's footsteps approaching.

"Hello, Michael. My name is Larry Reese. I'm from Guide Dogs for the Blind."

Mike let the jump rope drop. Mr. Reese had driven all the way to Palmdale from San Rafael, near San Francisco. An eight-hour drive just to see him.

"Nice to meet you, Mr. Reese." *Why would this man drive so far to visit me when I'm not even old enough for the program yet?*

"We're looking forward to having you come to the Guide Dogs campus to get a dog."

What? Didn't Sharon say I needed to be 16?

"You're all signed up to attend the program this summer."

Mike got the sudden urge to do something really childish like jump up and down screaming. How had such a great thing happened? To him?

It turned out that Mike's parents had applied for a dog. While Guide Dogs still required students to be 16, they made an exception for Mike. He never asked why Mom and Dad did it without telling him. He had a feeling they kept it a secret so he wouldn't be disappointed if Guide Dogs turned down his application.

Thoughts of how he would spend his summer consumed Mike's thoughts. School couldn't end fast enough.

♥ 🐕 ♥ 🐕 ♥

Before school even let out, Mike prepared for four weeks away from home. In late June, Mom and Dad dropped Ellery off at Scout camp, then drove Mike to San Rafael. Mike sat in the backseat wiggling like a four-year-old. He wasn't at all worried about getting homesick. He'd been to summer camp several times, and the thrill of getting a dog erased all nervousness.

As they drove up the gravel road to the campus, Mike realized that, until now, he'd hardly been outside Southern California. Mom tried to describe what she said was a beautiful lush campus surrounded by rolling green hills.

They arrived on a Sunday. Mike and his parents spent part of that day exploring the 11-acre school. A huge administration building stood at the front of campus, with the dormitory for students on one side of it. The dorm had eight double rooms. There was a dining room, a common room complete with TV and out-of-tune piano, and a swimming pool. The dog kennels were at the back. Is my dog waiting for me there?

At around 4:30 p.m., Mike settled into his room and met his roommate, John. Mike discovered that John was only two years older. John lived in Northern California. It felt good to know he wouldn't be the only teenager in class. He'd heard that most of his classmates would be adults.

He was thrilled to find that his room had a Talking Books player. Mike and John talked about their schools and their interests and what they expected the next four weeks to be like. They talked until the dinner bell rang. The building was so large that students might not hear the bell from all the dorm rooms, so the bell had to be carried up and down the dorm hall. That first night, the class's head trainer, Mr. Jeff Locke, carried the bell.

When everyone sat down, Mike discovered something that did make him nervous—being so much younger than most of his fellow students. He had never been around so many adults, let alone blind adults with more experience than he had. One man he got to know pretty well was Howard Mackey, a counselor with the Department of Rehabilitation. Mike learned that Mr. Mackey's job included helping other blind people learn the skills required to get a job and get through college.

That first night at guide dog school, all the students got to know each other and listened to Mr. Locke and another instructor, Bruce Benzler, discuss what would be happening over the next month. Classes started the next day.

The first thing Mike learned was the history of Guide Dogs for the Blind. During World War II, someone got the idea of training shelter dogs to assist soldiers who had been blinded in the war. The first guide dog was a German shepherd named Blondie. In 1941, a man named Sergeant Leonard Foulk became the first graduate of the program.

The students were surprised to discover that they did not immediately start training with a dog. Instead, they began what the instructors called Juno training. A trainer held the harness, playing the part of an imaginary dog named Juno, while the student learned the proper footwork.

"The key is to always lead with your left foot so it is beside the dog's right paw."

It sounded easy until Mike tried it and discovered the coordination involved. He also learned commands and hand signals, starting with the very first command that a guide dog learns.

"Forward." Bruce Benzler demonstrated for Mike how to lead with his left foot while sweeping his right hand out.

He learned how to use the harness and leash, and he listened to lectures about obedience, correcting and praising a dog, and how to keep his dog healthy. One thing that Guide Dogs for the Blind made a big deal about was the idea of partnership, like when Sharon had explained how she and Nola were a team.

"You are actually the one in the lead," Mr. Benzler said. "The dog might be doing the seeing, but you are the one who needs to know where you are going and stay aware of your surroundings."

They talked about something called intelligent disobedience, where a dog disobeys a command in order to keep his person safe.

"For example," Mr. Benzler explained, "let's say you reach an intersection and think it is safe to cross because you don't hear any cars coming. Your dog, on the other hand, sees a bicyclist headed your way. When you say the command 'Forward,' he will disobey you and stay put until it's safe to cross."

Finally the day came that Mike all the other students had been waiting for: Day Three, Dog Day.

The room buzzed with excitement during the morning lecture. Mike listened intently, but only because they were talking about the dogs; otherwise his mind would have wandered.

The group headed to the dining room for a quick lunch. Mike could hardly eat. Did they assign me a boy or a girl?

Then everyone went to their rooms to wait. And wait. Mike pulled out his Talking Books machine to pass the time, but even the novel he'd checked out couldn't ease his anxiety.

"This is killing me." John tossed aside a Braille magazine.

"I know." Mike started to pace.

He'd been told the trainers put a lot of thought and planning into matching dogs with handlers, as the students were now called. Did they walk slowly or quickly? Were they young or older? Did they live in a big city or in a small town? Mike would receive a calm dog with the energy to keep up with an active teenage and navigate chaotic high school hallways.

He checked his Braille watch. *Are they still deciding on my dog?* Or maybe they'd decided it was mistake to make an exception for such a young kid and were saving him for last so they could break it to him that, instead of getting a dog, they were sending him home? Or maybe...

The knock on his door made him jump.

"Michael, it's your turn."

Mike followed Mr. Benzler. This was it. A woman from his class passed him in the hall, accompanied by her new companion.

Mr. Benzler led Mike into a small room. "Sit quietly in this chair while I go get your dog," he said. "His name is Squire. Squire is a dark-red golden retriever."

A golden retriever. Retrievers are supposed to be great dogs.

"He weighs about 64 pounds."

And he's big. Cool!

"Don't say anything when I let him in. Just wait in the chair and let him come to you. Are you ready?"

Mike's heart raced. "Ready."

What will happen if he doesn't like me? God, please let him like me.

Mr. Benzler opened the door and in walked Squire. Mike fought to sit still as Squire padded across the room, right over to him, and started sniffing him from toes to face. His hands ached to pet him, to feel that amazing silken golden retriever fur, but Mr. Benzler had said to stay still, so he obeyed. He could feel Squire's nose through his jeans. His soft fur tickled Mike's hand. *Wow, this is strange. But a good kind of strange.* He could tell by the smell that Squire had just had a bath. Just for me. Finally, Squire stopped sniffing and stood still at Mike's feet, panting in a "Hi-how-you-doin'" sort of way.

"It looks like you found a friend."

"Can I move now?" Mike asked, almost in a whisper.

Mr. Benzler chuckled. "Yes, Mike, you can move."

Mike's hands instantly reached for Squire's wavy coat. The dog didn't move an inch, allowing Mike to stroke his back and neck and ears. Squire's breath warmed Mike's face. His throat tightened as Squire moved closer and nestled into Mike's shirt.

Mike instinctively wrapped his arms around Squire's neck to give him a hug. Flea soap never smelled this good on Peewee.

"You can take Squire back to your room now so you can get to know each other."

Mike pulled back. "Okay." He kept his hand on Squire's back, stroking him, still taking in the reality that the wonderful creature beside him was actually his.

"Use the leash and tell him to heel."

Mike nodded and slipped his fingers through the loop at the end of the leash.

"Squire, heel." He tried hard to sound authoritative but nice.

The walk back to his room felt like walking on air, like he and Squire were a perfect fit. In September, he would walk down the hallways of Palmdale High School with Squire, and into scout meetings and church. Instead of standing out as different, he'd stand out as having a beautiful dog with him.

By the time Mike got to his room, his roommate was gone.

"Hey, Squire." Mike sat on the edge of his bed and unhooked Squire's leash. "What do you think of our room? Pretty neat, huh?"

Suddenly, things felt a bit awkward, like having a new friend over and realizing that you don't know what he likes to do? He did the only thing he could think of. Mike turned on the Talking Books machine. "You like Zane Gray westerns? I just started this one today so you haven't missed much."

Mike spent every moment of his remaining weeks on campus with Squire. He learned to read Squire's body language through the handle of his harness and soon realized that Squire could read his, too. As a class, the students learned to walk with their dogs around town, take buses, and cross streets. The first trip off campus, they went to a place called the Guide Dogs San Rafael Lounge, and Mike excused himself to go to the restroom.

"Uh, Mike," one of the other students said from the hallway as he was finishing up. "You might want to close the door."

Mike gasped and shut the door, his face hot with horror. Who had seen him? *This sure isn't like being at home.*

As he got to know his classmates, Mike met a few men and women who were classified as blind but actually had some sight. Unlike him, some saw shadows and shapes; some could even read print as long as it was large and they pulled it up close to their eyes. Some were gradually losing their sight to diseases; others had struggled to see since birth. The students who could see a little had an extra challenge—trusting the guide dog instead of relying on what little eyesight they had.

During the first few days that Mike worked with Squire, either Mr. Benzler or Mr. Locke walked right behind the new team, making suggestions and observing how Mike and his new friend bonded. Over time, the trainers moved farther away. At first, as the trainers lagged farther and farther behind during the walks, Squire would look back, trying to see those who'd worked with him for so many months. Eventually, the trainers stopped following the students. Mike and his classmates were permitted to create their own routes so long as they remained within a certain distance from the lounge. The trainers observed from a distance. By this time Squire had gotten used to working with Mike and stopped looking for his trainers.

During the last week of class, the students boarded the Guide Dogs bus and traveled into San Francisco for work in a big city. While in San Francisco, Mike and Squire traveled around office buildings, through large shopping centers, and rode a famous San Francisco cable car. All of these activities were designed to get the team used to working together in a wide variety of situations, to help them bond, and to prepare for the day they would leave the school and go off into their everyday lives together. Mike never grew tired of traveling with Squire. As they walked, he could hear people commenting on what a beautiful dog he had and what a great job he was doing for such a young person. For once, he was traveling with a group of friends instead of tagging along with his older brother or walking alone. He felt himself beginning to walk taller, knowing that wherever he went, it would be him and Squire.

By the time graduation day came, Mike felt like he and Squire could do just about anything together.

Mom and Dad were not able to return for graduation day. Instead Mike would have his first new adventure with Squire. They were going to take an airplane flight back home.

But first, he sat with the other students sat on a platform as, one by one, those who had raised the dogs as puppies officially presented them to their new owners. When it was Mike's turn, Nancy Nichol, a student and member of a 4-H club in Stockton, California, handed Squire over to Mike.

Mike graduated on July 25, 1964. One student was selected to speak for the entire class. On this day, that speaker would be Mike, who had been chosen as class valedictorian. Mike talked about Squire and all the other new guide dogs.

"This is the greatest day of my life," he told the audience of puppy raisers, trainers, and interested San Rafael residents. "I know that I—that all of us—

will live up to the responsibility we have been given to work with, care for, and love these new friends that have been handed to us."

Mike left campus that day, not just with a dog, but with a new best friend.

After graduation Mike was driven to the airport where he boarded an airplane to fly to Burbank Airport, the closest commercial airport to Palmdale. Mike and Squire were put in the lounge area of the Conair C4 aircraft. Mike sat on a couch facing toward the center of the plane. The stewardesses thought this place would give Squire the most room to lie at his master's feet. Many years later, Mike learned that there were safer places for Squire. But on this first trip, Mike didn't care where he sat. The kid whose parents had once been told, "He won't be able to do anything for himself" had just become the youngest student ever to graduate from Guide Dogs for the Blind. Now he was flying home without anyone holding his hand, with his partner in independence resting at his feet.

9

MAKING THE CUT

Roselle, 1999

Roselle turned right and between a pair of cones. She saw another pair on her left and wove through them.

"Good girl." Her trainer, Todd Jurek, reached down and rubbed between Roselle's ears. "You are doing great."

Since returning to the Guide Dogs for the Blind campus, Roselle had worked with Todd every day on obedience training, with commands like *heel, sit*, and *stay*. The first official guide command Roselle learned was *forward*. Each exercise began with *forward*, a guide dog's prompt to start walking.

Right, left, stop, and *hop up* came next. "Hop up" means to go faster, pay attention, get back to work, or get closer to something, not that she got to jump on the person giving the command. Instead of a puppy coat, she now wore a larger Guide Dog in Training vest, and added a harness to her working uniform. The harness was now her cue to go to work. When the harness came off, she could relax, play, and let people pet her.

Roselle's life was a lot busier now than during her puppy days with the Sterns. She still took trips around town, but they were about more than socialization and learning to behave properly in stores, church, and parks. While out with Todd or one of the volunteers, she practiced important skills like walking her trainer in a straight line, stopping at each curb, and recognizing when it was safe to cross a street. Her progress was constantly evaluated. Every few weeks, she needed to pass what they called a benchmark or phase. These tests revealed whether she was advancing like she should. She had passed every one so far without a single problem. Altogether she would need to pass 10 benchmarks. Only the best dogs made it through the entire course.

Some dogs arrived at Guide Dogs for the Blind around the same time as Roselle only to be cut early on, but Roselle fit right in, enjoying every moment of her life on campus. As Kay predicted, she had many friends both dog and human, and each day brought a new challenge.

A quiver of excitement raced through Roselle whenever Todd strapped on her leash and harness. This meant it was time to learn something new, practice an important command, or go somewhere exciting like downtown San Rafael. The training exercises weren't always easy, and sometimes they did the same thing over and over and over again so the skill or command would become as natural as taking a breath, but she loved working with Todd. It didn't seem to matter that he had other dogs to train during the day; when Roselle's turn came, she got his full attention.

Roselle had heard Todd tell other trainers that she had a lot of confidence and showed promise. Whatever those words meant, Todd looked pleased when he said them, spurring Roselle on to work even harder for him.

Today, Roselle and Todd were working on avoiding obstacles. Todd gripped the handle of the harness that a blind person would hold and Roselle watched for the cones. Roselle stayed just ahead of Todd, always on his left. The goal was to lead Todd through each pair of cones without running him into any of them.

The last pair was very close together, making them difficult to squeeze through and around. Her paw barely touched the bottom of the cone on her right. Did Todd hit the cone on his side?

When she heard, "Good job, Roselle!" she knew he hadn't.

Roselle wagged her tail hard as Todd praised her. He popped a piece of kibble in her mouth as a reward. *Yum!* Unlike with her puppy raisers, the trainers on campus often used treats when teaching new skills.

After a quick break, Todd rearranged the cones, positioning some in places that forced Roselle to step up and down a curb.

Across the yard, another trainer sent one of Roselle's friends—a black Lab named Sage—between two parallel bars that dead-ended at a wall. Once Sage reached the wall, he needed to back out of the bars immediately, proving that he could move a person back and out of harm's way. Roselle tried to keep her focus on the cones instead of on her friend. Distractions were still a challenge for her, although Todd said she was improving.

Sage stopped at the wall and tried to turn around instead of backing up. Several dogs had been dropped since Roselle arrived. If Sage didn't master those bars pretty soon, he could get dropped too. It would be sad to see Sage go. He was a nice dog.

I can't blame him for panicking a little. Those bars made me feel trapped the first few times Todd took me through them, until I realized I wasn't trapped at all; I just needed to back up.

Roselle forced her eyes to watch for the cones instead of worrying about poor Sage. She reached the end of the course and stopped. Todd reached into his pocket, held out another piece of kibble, and praised her good work. He rubbed her head and neck.

Good teacher, Roselle said with her large brown eyes, nestling into Todd's hand.

That was the end of her afternoon workout with Todd. Tomorrow they might do something different, like walk on the treadmill or practice avoiding what Todd called low-lying objects. For that, someone would hold a bar or stick that represented a tree branch, pipe, or some other thing that could hang low and cause injury to a blind person who didn't see it coming. Roselle needed to stop in front of the object, preventing Todd from hitting it. At first, they held the bar just above nose level, then raised it higher and higher. Roselle was not the only dog in school who found low-lying objects difficult. Walking with her head up instead of nose to the ground was hard enough; looking up felt completely unnatural. The more they practiced, the more quickly she spotted the bar. Todd hadn't been whacked in the face yet.

Yesterday she had mastered the command "find the trash can," a skill that required her to memorize where the trash can in Todd's office was located and lead him to it. When she got matched with a blind person, he or she might need Roselle to find specific things like the mailbox or a newspaper. While crossing streets, she needed to learn to find the pole for the traffic signal, so this kind of recall was extremely important.

Finding things is fun, kind of like playing Hide and Seek with Ted and Kay, only I'm seeking something instead of hiding.

Some days, Roselle got to hang out with Todd in his office. He had a cool chair on wheels that swiveled all the way around. He kept toys in his office, including a wonderful rope for Tug of War. That was her new favorite game.

One rainy morning, Todd swiveled his desk chair around and tossed the rope toy her way. Roselle pounced and caught the rope before it hit the floor. Tail swishing, she ran back to Todd, tightening her grip as Todd tried to pull the toy from her mouth. Todd tugged, but Roselle pulled harder.

Roselle breathed hard through her nostrils, determined not to let the rope go.

Todd rested his feet on the bar at the bottom on his chair, and as soon as he did, Roselle gave the rope a good hard yank. She backed up, taking Todd and his chair with her.

Roselle's eyes bore into Todd's. *Pull the Trainer is*

even better than Tug-of-War.

Todd laughed and let her pull him all the way to the office door.

"Look at you. You're no wimp, that's for sure!" Todd set his feet back on the floor. He gave Roselle's ears a quick rub. "Okay, that's enough. Leave it. Round One? Roselle."

Roselle dropped the end of her rope. She panted from the wonderful surge of adrenaline, silently begging for another round. *Please, Todd. That was so much fun. Again, again!*

"I'm afraid Round Two will have to wait until tomorrow."

Disappointed, Roselle went to a dog bed in Todd's office and lay down. She promptly settled in for a nap.

"There she goes, snoring again," Roselle overheard Todd say as she drifted off. "Roselle, you are one of the best snorers I have ever met, and I know some pretty loud humans."

After a half hour, Todd woke Roselle to take her back to her kennel while he worked on his other duties. A new group of students was waiting to receive guide dogs. Todd was extra busy today, finishing up the process of matching dogs with students. Roselle had watched many students come and go from campus since Ted and Kay dropped her off, and she'd seen older dogs trade in their training vests for official guide dog attire.

By the next evening, every student on campus walked with a dog instead of a cane. On her way to train with Todd, Roselle watched a middle-aged woman and a teenage girl stroll down one of the tree-lined paths. The younger girl looked taller than she had on the first day. The older woman smiled more. Did meeting their dogs make them that happy? She recognized their dogs, Taz and Uriah. They looked different too, like they were doing what they had been born to do.

"Pretty soon, that'll be you." Todd patted Roselle's back. "I've known since Day One that you were a natural, and you are. Just keep up the good work."

Roselle watched the two new teams find a place to sit on the grass. Uriah and the teenage girl flowed so gracefully together that they almost seemed like one person.

"All you need to do is pass your final tests next week."

10

DOGS ALLOWED

Mike, 1964-1965

"Hi, Mike. Hi Squire," Cindy said as she passed Mike in the hallway on his first day at Palmdale High School. "Oops. Sorry, I forgot about not talking to your dog when he has his harness on."

"It's okay, this time." Mike clicked his tongue to locate the door to algebra class. Squire walked obediently at his left. "I have a little more patience for girls who teach me important skills like bike riding."

"Well, at least I didn't try to pet him this time."

"Yes, you're learning faster than most kids."

So far, Mike's classes were going well. He only had one that was a bit of a disappointment—General Science. Sure, it was only the first day, but from the sound of the outline, they would be covering the same old basic stuff that he already knew. Ellery was taking chemistry. Too bad he couldn't transfer to that class. Hopefully, Algebra 1 would be more interesting.

Mike found a desk in the front row.

"Squire, down," he said quietly. Squire found his place beside Mike's desk. When the bell to start class rang, the dog didn't even flinch.

"That kid has a dog in class," the boy behind him said.

"Aw, he's cute." A girl across the aisle squatted down. "Can I pet him?"

"Not right now, sorry." Mike still felt a little uncomfortable turning down requests to pet Squire or give him snacks. He explained the rules.

The girl backed away. "Sorry, I didn't know. Well, he's a really pretty dog."

"Thanks." Mike smiled. Even if he couldn't allow his classmate to distract Squire from his work, the attention from having a regal golden retriever at his side wasn't bad at all.

"Good morning, students," the teacher raised her voice over the clamor of students. "My name is Mrs. Duffy, and I will be your teacher for Algebra 1." She took roll quickly and explained the class policies then got right down to business. "Okay, let's get started on the exciting world of algebra."

The groans behind him told Mike that many in the

class did not consider algebra exciting at all.

Mrs. Duffy started writing something on the board. "Who can tell me the value of x in this equation?"

Mike lifted his hand.

"Yes."

Mike detected the shift in Mrs. Duffy's voice, from assured to nervous.

"Can you please describe what is on the board?"

"Um, certainly. I wrote, if x plus y equals five and y equals three."

"Thank you." Another guy answered the question before Mike could figure it out in his head. He couldn't help feeling sorry for Mrs. Duffy. He had already been warned that algebra was very visual because it involved lots of written equations and reading the blackboard. It must be even more difficult for the teacher trying to explain it to a kid who couldn't see, since it forced her to describe what she was writing, something she didn't normally do. But Mrs. Duffy did such a good job and had such a great attitude that Mike gained immediate respect for her.

As the weeks passed, however, Mike found that life in Mrs. Duffy's class was harder than he expected it to be on that first day. Not that Algebra 1 was difficult, but when it came to test taking Mrs. Duffy demanded that students write out all their answers and "be sure to show all your work." Mike was used to doing math in his head. The only way he could show his work was to write his answers in Braille, which Mrs. Duffy couldn't read.

Sometimes Mrs. Duffy asked Mike to recite the answers to her test questions, but when Mike answered, she deducted points even when he got the correct answer. He could describe what he was thinking and how he solved the problem, but to Mrs. Duffy, that wasn't the same as writing the steps out on paper. The battle only added to his frustration of standing out as different. *Can't she see I know what I am doing?*

One day, Mike decided to try an experiment. He wrote all the answers to an assignment in Braille and turned in his paper with the other students.

Immediately, Mrs. Duffy held up Mike's paper. "Class, Mike showed all his work. Congratulations Mike."

"Good job, Mike." The guy behind Mike thumped his shoulder.

Mrs. Duffy had no idea whether Mike really answered the math problems or not, and he knew it; the teacher simply took his word for it.

Mike still got a "C" on the assignment.

Knowing that Mrs. Duffy had a nice side kept Mike from getting too angry with her. One day, for instance, a piano from the music room got moved to Mrs. Duffy's classroom while waiting for a repair. She set down her chalk.

"It seems like a shame to let that beautiful instrument sit there. Does anyone play piano?"

"I do," a girl in the back row said.

"Would you like to play something for us?"

"Sure."

Mike was so awestruck by how well the girl played that he wished he'd developed his own musical skills more.

A guy who was known for goofing off in class played next. He amazed everyone even more.

Mrs. Duffy allowed the concert to continue the entire period. She didn't even assign homework that day. Mike held onto that memory when he got frustrated with her "show your work" policy.

❤ 🐈 ❤ 🐈 ❤

Halfway through the year, Mike got some relief from his boring science class, thanks to the interest he'd taken in ham radio.

He was doing extremely well in General Science, and the last part of the year would be devoted to electronics, Morse code, and other subjects that Mike had mastered while earning his radio licenses. He spent the last quarter of ninth grade in Senior Physics instead of General Science.

In physics, students learned how and why things moved and behaved as they did. They studied light and how our universe works. Through physics he learned the answers to such questions as "Why is the sky blue?" and "Why does the sound of a car change as it speeds past a person standing on a sidewalk?" Mike was fascinated. He even learned concepts that helped as he and his dad took and passed more advanced amateur radio license tests.

Then a day came when Mike got another visit during class, but this one wasn't nearly as exciting as when he learned he would be attending guide dog school.

Mike was in the middle of algebra class when an office assistant came in and handed Mrs. Duffy a slip.

"The assistant principal, Mr. Fisher, wants to see you, Mike." Mrs. Duffy excused Mike to go right away.

Mike's face flushed with dread and embarrassment as he and Squire headed to the office. No one ever gets called to the office for good news.

Mike sat in the hard chair across from the long desk. He didn't need to be able to see the desk to feel intimidated. Hearing Mr. Fisher clear his throat was enough.

"I'm afraid we have a problem, Mike," Mr. Fisher said.

Mike's shoulders tightened.

"I just got a call and apparently some members of the school board don't like the idea of you and Squire riding the school bus."

"But we've been riding it all year."

"I know. Unfortunately, they have a point. I have the school handbook here, and it reads 'No live animals of any kind are allowed on school buses.' I'm afraid you will not be permitted to take Squire on the bus anymore."

"But I am supposed to take Squire with me whenever I travel anywhere, including school. He doesn't cause any trouble. No one even notices him anymore." Once the newness of having a dog at school wore off, his classmates had gone back to discussing ordinary teenager stuff, like dances and dates and the latest movies. Without Squire, he would go back to being a loner.

"I know, but I don't make the rules."

Mike took a little comfort in the fact that Mr. Fisher didn't sound pleased with the news. Then he thought of something that might help his case.

"When I went to guide dog school, they gave me a card to show bus drivers and anyone who tried to turn me away because of Squire, reminding them of the laws."

Mr. Fisher was quiet for moment. "You have a good point. Perhaps your parents can call the school district and work something out, but for now, I'm afraid you can't ride the bus to school as long as Squire is with you."

Mike went home completely confused. *Someone must have made a mistake. They can't do this!*

But when he checked the Braille copy of the school handbook that an organization called Antelope Valley Braille Transcribers had printed for him, it was right there under his fingertips. Dogs could not ride the school bus.

"This is ridiculous," Dad fumed when he got home from work and heard the news. His irritation over the neighbors complaining about Mike riding his bike around town was nothing compared to his anger with the school board. He immediately called Mr. Fisher.

The assistant principal stood his ground. Even though they hadn't had a single complaint about Squire's behavior, the district planned to hire a driver to take Mike to and from Palmdale High.

Mom was equally upset. "Not only will that cost the district money," she pointed out, "but this goes against everything we have been trying to do—making sure Mike is treated like any other boy his age. This is unacceptable."

Peewee ran out from under the table and nipped at Squire's tail, starting their nightly ritual of chasing each other around the house. Even their antics didn't lighten the mood.

The next day, Dad requested a special meeting with the school board. In the meantime, Mike rode in a special car to school, feeling singled out and even more isolated than ever, while Dad researched the law at the Palmdale library.

The whole family attended the meeting, prepared for action and ready to win. The school board might have a lot of power, but they couldn't argue with the law, could they?

With a boldness that Mike had never seen before, his dad reminded the board that it was a felony to deny access to a blind person with a guide dog. "Someone could go to jail for this," Dad warned.

Mike tried not to smile. *Go Dad!*

The superintendent turned to the chairman of the school board, who worked as a lawyer by day. "Is this true?"

The lawyer nodded. "It is."

Mike rested his hand on Squire's head. Winning the rest of the board over would be a cinch.

The superintendent leaned back, took a deep breath, and tapped his pen. Then he straightened his shoulders. "Even so, we are talking about a school bus, not a city bus. School rules come first. Our decision stands."

Mike's mouth dropped open. This can't be happening.

No matter what the law said, Mike and Squire could not ride the school bus. The school board voted three-to-two in favor of the superintendent. Mike, Ellery, and his parents left the meeting in shock. Didn't the school board care that they were doing something wrong?

But Dad wasn't finished yet.

He went home and wrote a letter to the governor of California. Governor Edmund "Pat" Brown was known for opposing discrimination of any kind. Mr. Hingson explained the whole situation in his letter, ending it with, "The school board is discriminating against my son."

Not long after that, Mike and his parents heard that the superintendent had been called to a meeting with the governor.

"I wish I could be there to listen in." Mike tried to imagine the scene. "Talk about being called to the principal's office."

"Me too," Dad said.

A few days later, Mike got called to the assistant principal's office again.

"Well, Mike . . ."

Mike gripped Squire's harness, hoping he didn't look as nervous as he felt.

"You are back on the bus. Your dad made it happen."

He squeezed Mike's shoulder. Mike's relief came out in a smile that lasted until he returned to class.

The next morning, Mike eagerly boarded the bus with Squire.

"Welcome back," the bus driver said.

"I've never been so excited to ride the bus."

♥ 🐾 ♥ 🐾 ♥

Unfortunately, this triumph didn't end Mike's freshman year struggles. While Squire officially became an accepted member of Palmdale High School and Mike excelled in his physics class, Mrs. Duffy's firm policy on showing all work when solving equations continued to make Algebra 1 an endless source of frustration. Mike knew better than to expect an A, but his final grade sent shock waves through this high achiever.

"I got a C?" Mike almost shouted when Mom read his report card to him. "That is so unfair. I've been doing algebra with Dad since I was six. I know that stuff!"

"We know you know it," Mom assured him. "I bet even Mrs. Duffy does. She's probably just afraid to bend the rules. You know the old saying, 'If I do it for you, I'll have to do it for everyone.' At least the class is over, and next year, you'll be in a different class."

He spent the summer thinking about how he might work better with his geometry teacher.

On the first day of his sophomore year, Mike chose a place in the front row of geometry class and Squire prepared to nap at his feet.

"My name is Mr. Herboldsheimer," the teacher told the class. "I'm a new teacher here at Palmdale."

Mike heard him scratch his long name on the blackboard.

"Don't worry; you can call me Mr. Herbo." Not only was Mr. Herbo new to Palmdale High, this was his first year of teaching. Before going back to college, he had worked for the Natural Gas Company in Nebraska.

Geometry started out a lot like Algebra 1. Mr. Herbo drew a triangle on the board, along with an equation. Mike raised his hand and asked him to describe it. Mr. Herbo hesitated a bit but gave such a detailed description that Mike solved the problem. Mr. Herbo was nothing like Mrs. Duffy. This new teacher worked closely with Mike and clearly wanted him to succeed. When it came time to take tests, Mr. Herbo worked with Mike after school. There, he drew the shape for each problem on an erasable slate, took Mike's finger, and traced it along the raised line before reading the test question out loud.

"Now, tell me the answer."

Mr. Herbo waited patiently as Mike worked each problem out in his head and gave his answer orally.

Mike not only considered Mr. Herbo his favorite teacher ever, but he began to see him as a friend. One day, they were in the library when Cindy walked by.

"Happy Birthday, Mike."

Mike grinned. "Thank you."

"Is it your birthday?" Mr. Herbo shut the geometry book. "We need to celebrate."

A half hour later, they were standing in line at Foster's Freeze ordering banana splits. They found a table and Mike waited there with Squire while Mr. Herbo got their ice cream and brought it back to the table.

"You just received a compliment, Mike." Mr. Herbo sat down. "The man taking our order had no idea you were blind until he saw you walking with Squire."

"Really? Thanks, that is a compliment."

Mike had worked very hard at learning to "look people in the eye," knowing that was the polite thing to do. For him, this meant looking in the direction that he knew a person's eyes were, judging by the sound of his or her voice. Often, the milky tone of his light blue eyes gave away his blindness, even though they looked completely normal otherwise. But today, it hadn't. If felt great to know the guy at the counter had seen him as just another teenager ordering ice cream.

They spent the next hour talking about what they enjoyed doing when they weren't studying geometry. Mike told his teacher all about his ham radio license.

Mr. Herbo was so interested that Mike offered to show him his equipment. A couple weeks later, Mr. Herbo gave Mike a ride home so he could see it.

Mike's Mom greeted them at the door. "Hello, Mr. Herbo."

"Good afternoon, Mrs. Hingson. I'm just here to see Mike's laboratory. I mean his radio equipment."

Mike let Squire off his harness. Peewee immediately ran over to pester Squire, triggering a game of chase down the hallway and through the living room.

"The room is back here." His parents had let him use a spare room for his setup. Mike didn't even need to feel his way to the table where he kept everything. He knew this room by heart.

He picked up the radio receiver. "See, if you talk into this, you can contact anyone in the world. I've talked to people in . . ." Mike stopped, realizing Mr. Herbo hadn't made it past the doorway.

"Uh, Mike." Mr. Herbo chuckled.

"Yeah? You okay, sir?" Hopefully, he wasn't sick or something. He'd been dying to show off his stuff and demonstrate how it all worked.

"I'm fine, it's just, well . . . Do you happen to have a light in here?"

Mike froze. Oops.

"Oh, yeah." Mike made his way over to the light switch that he never used unless Ellery or one of his parents was in the room. "Sorry, Mr. Herbo. I forgot you could see."

Mr. Herbo laughed and patted Mike's back. "I guess we're even then, because I often forget that you can't."

11

COUNTDOWN TO DOG DAY

Roselle, 1999

Roselle waited beside the Guide Dogs for the Blind van as Todd pulled a blindfold from his jacket pocket. A man named Kelly Martin, one of the supervisors from campus, jotted notes down on a clipboard. The big day had come. Roselle was beginning her final tests to become a guide dog.

Todd secured the blindfold around his eyes and buttoned his jacket. Roselle shivered a little under a chilly November wind.

During each test, Todd would play the role of a blind man while Kelly followed them and acted as a spotter, noting how well Roselle obeyed commands, guided, and kept Todd out of danger. In her 20 weeks of training at the campus, Roselle had passed every evaluation and Todd continued to rave about her progress, but that did not make her final tests any less important. If she failed one of them, she could still be cut from the program.

For her first test, Roselle needed to guide Todd through a busy area of downtown San Rafael.

Roselle focused intently on her surroundings. They were in the parking lot outside the Guide Dogs lounge, which meant guiding Todd to the street while also staying aware of cars coming from behind, backing out of parking spaces, and turning from one row to another. Roselle perked up her ears, preparing to listen and watch for things that Todd couldn't see and feel for the vibrations of approaching vehicles.

"We're ready," Todd told the spotter.

"Go for it." Kelly positioned himself behind Todd and Roselle.

"Okay, Roselle," Todd gripped the harness. "Forward."

Roselle guided Todd along the edges of the parking spaces, toward the exit then waited for him to tell her which way to turn.

"Left," Todd said.

Roselle took a left turn without hesitation.

Men and women hurried up and down the sidewalk; most of them didn't notice the pretty, unusually well behaved yellow Lab. She guided Todd around a cluster of ladies sipping coffee in front of a shop with delicious smells wafting out of it. One of the ladies smiled at Roselle; another stared at Todd as he walked blindfolded, but Roselle didn't stop or look back, even as the scents of pastries and muffins filled her nostrils.

The purpose of this first test was to check Roselle's ability to guide while surrounded by distractions. Todd was familiar with the area, so he knew where he was going. Roselle's job was to keep him from running into people, trash cans, or other objects, listen for his directions, and get him safely across streets and through areas that might be difficult for someone with very poor vision or no sight at all.

They walked on congested sidewalks, went in and out of shops, crossed streets, dodged a mailbox, and strolled through a park. Buses pulled into stops, kids cried, people talking on cell phones swerved around them, and impatient drivers honked their horns, but not once did Roselle lose concentration, get startled, or miss a command. She even kept Todd from hitting a dangling broken tree branch. Before she knew it, they were back in the parking lot and Todd was taking off his blindfold to read the spotter's notes.

"You guys did great," Kelly told Todd. "She didn't have any problems at all."

Roselle whipped her tail back and forth, gazing up

at Todd for approval.

"I knew you could do it." Todd cupped her face in his hands. "Just three more to go."

Roselle soaked up Todd's praise. I passed my first test, and it wasn't very hard at all!

Next, they took the traffic test. Todd and Kelly drove to a section of town that required crossing several intersections. Roselle not only needed to stop at each curb and recognize when it was safe to cross, but Kelly would also check her ability to hold Todd back from danger.

"Find the pole," Todd told Roselle, cuing her to locate the traffic light.

Todd pushed the button for the walk signal while Roselle watched the cars whizzing past her. When the vehicles traveling parallel to them had the right of way, Roselle knew it was their turn to cross. Before stepping off the curb, she paused to listen for cars that might sneak up on them from around the corner. She didn't hear or see any, so she led Todd off the curb and across the street, careful to avoid colliding with people crossing from the other side.

Intersections were still a bit scary, especially when drivers broke the rules, but that one had been a breeze.

The next intersection looked like it would be easy as well, with hardly any traffic and a light that turned after almost no wait at all, but before Roselle got ready to step off, she heard something.

"Forward." Todd swept his arm out again.

She didn't move. Something isn't right.

Sure enough, a small car with a very quiet engine made a right turn without slowing down. Roselle ignored the jump in her heart and waited for the car to pass before stepping off the curb.

Todd let out a sigh of relief.

At the next intersection, a motorcyclist ran a yellow light to make a turn when they were only halfway across. Roselle abruptly stepped back just before it zoomed in front of her, forcing Todd to stop in his tracks in the middle of the crosswalk, just in time to avoid being struck.

She focused all the harder and continued across, telling herself to let that near miss go.

"Whoa," Kelly told Todd when they reached the other side. "You don't want to know how close that was."

"But she sure proved herself." Todd continued down the street.

By the time they returned to the van, Roselle was exhausted from the concentration and frightening close calls. But she had passed another difficult part of her final, including facing unexpected surprises. Not only had she proven her obedience skills, she had also demonstrated intelligent disobedience.

The next day, Todd took her to a less dangerous

but just as critical location.

Northgate Shopping Mall was Guide Dog for the Blind's choice for testing their dogs inside a building that attracted a lot of people. The mall allowed Roselle to navigate crowds, ride elevators, guide up and down stairs, and use the escalator. Whether Roselle was matched with a young woman who enjoyed shopping or a businessman who worked in a large office, she would need all of these skills.

Roselle bounded up a long flight of stairs to the second floor of one of the main department stores.

One the way back down to the first floor, they took the escalator. Todd had trained her on the moving stairs many times, but getting herself and a person on safely was still a challenge. Once she was assigned to a handler, that person would already have some experience in riding escalators. Still, Roselle needed to show Todd and Kelly that she had mastered the process of stepping on, staying put until they reached the bottom, and stepping off without slips or hesitations that could cause the human holding her harness to trip and get hurt. Customers edged their way around Roselle, Todd, and Kelly, anxious to reach the bottom. Roselle watched them. *Why are humans always in such a hurry?*

"Let's head to the food court next," Todd told Kelly as they left the store.

Oh no, Roselle panted a little harder, *not the food*

court. Would the temptations of food ever get easier? Whether it did or not, her future handler would most likely take her to one at some point, so she needed to prove that she could sit through a lunch or dinner without snatching food off the table, getting in the way of customers carrying overloaded trays, or stopping to lick up a spilled milkshake. She had come a long way since the days when Kay purposely left bits of meat in the middle of the kitchen floor and forced her to practice leaving it alone, but that didn't mean she wasn't capable of slipping up.

The heavenly array of burgers, corn dogs, Chinese food, and pizza called to Roselle long before they entered. She hadn't eaten since early that morning. *Everything smells so good.*

A woman hurried toward the seating area with a tray of spaghetti. Suddenly the pasta didn't matter nearly as much as the fact that that woman would run into Todd if they didn't take a quick right turn. Roselle swerved as the woman took a step back.

"Oops, sorry about that."

They stopped beside a table where a man dropped a piece of lemon chicken. Roselle looked at it.

Leave it, she commanded herself. *Good girl.*

Todd directed her to exit the court and go to the elevator. Finally, she was free of that maze of temptations.

The elevator is down the hallway, right outside the

food court, she recalled, so she guided Todd there.

While waiting for the elevator, Roselle encountered another challenge; this time the challenge had ponytails and sat in a stroller.

"Doggie." The little girl giggled. She reached out. Her fingertips touched Roselle's right ear, triggering a desire to play instead of work. Children were so fun, especially children who liked dogs instead of getting scared and crying. Roselle thought about Todd and her harness and kept her eyes on the elevator door.

"No, no." The little girl's mom gently pulled her hand away. "Don't touch strange doggies."

"This dog is in school right now," Todd told her. "No touching, please."

She pointed at Todd's blindfold. "Peekaboo!"

Roselle wagged her tail. She sneaked a peak at the child's chubby-cheeked face then turned her focus back to the elevator door. Todd needed her to watch for when it opened.

The mother whisked her daughter away as the door opened. "We need to let that doggie do his work."

Roselle led Todd and Kelly into the elevator. A cluster of teenage girls huddled in the corner whispering and laughing. They stopped laughing for a moment as Todd felt for the button, but as soon as Roselle turned around to face the door, the girls started cracking up again. One of the girls backed into Roselle and lost her footing, almost sitting on Roselle's back.

"I'm so sorry!" She stopped laughing and straightened herself up. One of the other girls gasped, another laughed even harder.

Roselle peered up at the girl. She looks sorry. Roselle quickly adjusted her feet and resisted the urge to turn around and make friends with the girls.

"You better get away from that dog," one of the other girls warned. "That's a guide dog. If you touch one, I think you get fined or something."

"I would not get fined. My grandma raises service dogs. I know the rules."

The door opened and Roselle headed out, followed by Todd and Kelly.

"I can't remember the last time we had two near disasters so close together," Kelly said as he wrote.

"Yeah, good save, Roselle." Todd directed Roselle to head toward the exit. "I'd say you mastered the mall."

Back at the Guide Dogs campus, Todd tested Roselle's recall of everyday commands and obedience. He asked her to do things that a blind person might request, like sit, stay, or heel. He reviewed old commands, checking her position and the quickness of her response. Then he took her back to her kennel for the night.

Roselle immediately curled up on her bed. Did she

pass or fail? At the moment, she was too tired to care. When Todd came to get her the next morning, she expected him to take her to the van and drive downtown for another test. Instead, they went to his office.

"Well, Roselle . . ." Todd sat in his chair with the wheels on it.

Roselle glanced at Todd's tugging rope. Time to play?

No, he looked too serious. *Is something wrong?* No, she didn't sense any sadness or tension coming from her trainer.

Todd rolled his chair closer. Then he gave Roselle a hug. "You did it! You passed! Congratulations, girl, you're a guide dog."

Todd pulled back and smiled. Roselle gave him a doggie grin.

I'm a guide dog?

I did it! I'm a guide dog!

"I knew on the very first day that you would pass."

If it hadn't been against the rules, she would have jumped up on Todd and licked his face. Instead she settled for wagging her tail, sitting up straight and tall, and enjoying the pride on her trainer's face.

She had done what only half of her fellow guide dog puppies accomplished—made it through every stage of training. Any day now, she could be matched with a blind man, woman, or teenager. *Will it happen today?*

♥ 🐕 ♥ 🐕 ♥

The next day, Roselle was still waiting. She walked with Todd; she practiced commands; she played with her friends in the kennel, but no one said a thing about her exciting new assignment. A week later, she still didn't have a person. A group of blind students arrived to train with guide dogs, and Roselle continued to wait. No one had forgotten about her or changed their mind; Todd and the other trainers simply needed to decide on the right match, knowing how important it was to pair the perfect dog with each man or woman.

Another group of students arrived. Some rode in on airport shuttles driven by campus staff; others were dropped off by their parents, husbands, wives, or grown children. As always, their mix of excitement and nerves made the campus vibrate.

While Roselle walked the grounds with Todd, the men and women took a tour of the campus designed especially for new students. For the first few days of school, the students took classes and Roselle only saw them when they were on breaks. One older man seemed to know the place extremely well, like he had been there before. He was friendly and called many of the staff members by name. He even showed other students around. *He had—what was that word that Todd always used? Confidence. That was it! That man had a lot of confidence.*

Roselle watched him from a distance as he sat on a bench talking to a younger man, showing him some kind of electronic device. One thing Roselle noticed was that blind people had a lot of interesting gadgets—Braille and talking watches, balls that beeped when they threw them, screens that made pictures and words look larger.

The older man looked very proud of the device in his hand, and he looked smart too. At the same time, he seemed like the type of person who would enjoy playing Tug-of-War with her.

"Come, Roselle." Todd led her away from the man. "I want to introduce you to someone."

They passed two women who stood near the administration building talking. Something about Dog Day. According to these women, it was happening tomorrow and neither of them expected to get much sleep because of it.

When will my turn for Dog Day come?

Todd took Roselle to an office down the hall from his, where one of the other trainers worked.

"Hey, Dave." Todd knocked on the open door before entering. "I have a visitor for you."

Dave held a hand out to Roselle. "Hello, Roselle. Welcome to my family."

What did he mean, "Welcome to my family?" Dave

couldn't be her new person. He wasn't blind. She had seen him training other dogs.

As Todd and Dave talked, Roselle learned what was happening. Instead of staying in Todd's group, she was being assigned to one of Dave Byerly's students.

"Roselle is definitely the right match for him," Todd told Dave.

Him? Roselle cocked her head to one side. *Him who?*

"I agree." Dave nodded and rubbed Roselle's neck. "She has all the qualities he is looking for."

Roselle looked from Dave to Todd. She didn't want to leave his group. Dave seemed nice, but Todd was her trainer—her friend. Being a guide dog sure did include a lot of goodbyes.

But Dave and Todd both looked so excited that Roselle couldn't help getting a little thrilled as well. *Something good is about to happen. I can tell.*

"I'll take her to the groomers then she's all yours." Todd leaned down. "You hear that, Roselle? Tomorrow, you meet your person."

12

CAMPUS, CARS, AND KIDNAPPINGS

Mike, 1968-1972

In September 1968, Mike's mom and dad did something that few would have expected 18 years earlier when they learned their baby boy was blind. They dropped their grown-up son off at college.

Despite his struggle in Algebra 1 and the extra work required to learn and take tests in classrooms designed for sighted students, Mike earned top grades and was on the honor roll throughout high school. Outside of school, he earned the rank of Eagle Scout.

During his junior year, Mike and his parents had visited the University of California Irvine (UCI) campus and met the head of the physics department,

Dr. Ford, who didn't hesitate a bit about having a blind student in his program. Mike applied, was accepted, and chose physics as his major.

As thrilled as Mike's parents were over his acceptance, Mike knew it was difficult for them to let him go. But they kept to themselves whatever fears stirred inside, allowing their son to spread his wings and head off into the adult world. Their hard work and insistence that Mike be raised and treated like a regular kid had paid off. Mike was surpassing their dreams.

Mike battled some mixed feelings of his own. He couldn't wait to trade the halls of Palmdale High for college, but leaving home meant stepping out into the adult world. He had always been brave. He was brave enough to ride a bike when he couldn't see, go away to guide dog school, and speak up when he needed teachers to read what was written on the blackboard. He chose UCI because he liked the idea of attending a newer school and had received such a warm reception when he visited. But the University of California Irvine campus was huge with more students and teachers than there were people in Palmdale. Instead of being one of 30 kids in a classroom, he might be one of 100 or more.

He would no longer have Mom and Dad to fight for him against unfair rules, or a big brother to hang out with. Ellery attended California State University

Fullerton, which wasn't far away from Mike's college, but that wasn't the same as seeing his brother every day. Graduating meant saying goodbye to Mr. Herbo and neighborhood kids like Cindy. But he had one thing that the other freshmen didn't—he had Squire at his side to walk through every moment with him.

Mike and Squire spent the summer after graduation attending a special program at UC Santa Cruz for blind students who were about to enter college. There, Mike learned a skill that he skipped while growing up; he learned to use a white cane. Instead of walking with Squire, he tapped the long collapsible stick in front of him to locate curbs, doorways, bumps in the road, or obstacles like mailboxes, trashcans, and bikes. The cane also told drivers and people who happen to be walking by, "This person can't see you." It felt strange at first to hold a stick instead of Squire's harness. Mike suddenly wished he'd learned to use a cane earlier in life like most other blind people. What if I am the only one who doesn't know what I'm doing? But he caught onto cane travel within minutes. Before he knew it, he was joining the rhythmic taps of the dozens of other canes on campus.

Using a cane wasn't the only new thing Mike discovered that summer; for the first time he was in a program made up completely of blind teenagers and young adults. He met guys and girls from all over the state and from all kinds of backgrounds. Many of the students, like him, had been treated like ordinary kids, going to regular schools and participating in activities that any other boy or girl their age would enjoy. They played musical instruments, served in student government, and went to the prom; some left Mike envying their active social lives. Then there were those who had been sheltered since birth. That, he couldn't relate to at all. One girl had gone her entire childhood without doing chores, so the kitchen staff and students needed to remind her almost daily to clear her tray after meals in the dining hall. A guy Ellery's age had never spent more than one night away from his parents. At first, Mike and his new friends looked down on these kids. When would they grow up? How would they ever survive in the real world?

One night, Mike and a bunch of his friends were playing a game with Braille cards and started telling stories of crazy things they did as kids. Mike told the group about his paper route and the dog on Sumac Street that was trained to fetch the paper.

The girl who always left her tray on the table interrupted. "You had a paper route?"

"Sure." Mike suddenly missed those days of riding the tandem bike with Ellery. "I shared it with my brother, but believe me, he made sure I did my share of the work."

"That sounds like so much fun. I asked my parents for a bike once, but they said it was too dangerous, even when my sister promised to stay by my side the whole time."

Mike tried to imagine how he would have responded if his parents said no to him riding a bike, running to the candy store with his cousins, or pursuing his interest in building a radio. *Would I have begged them to change their minds, felt gypped, or just accepted it because I didn't know any better?*

How different would my life be if I'd been born into another family, to parents who didn't treat my brother and me exactly alike? Maybe instead of looking down on those sheltered kids, I should thank God for giving me such courageous, amazing parents.

The summer whizzed by, and soon Mike's parents were helping him get settled in his dorm room at college.

Mike spent the first few weeks learning every inch of the 1,500-acre campus, first with his cane, then with Squire, then with his bike. He learned alternate routes to his classes, the library, the dorms, the dining hall, and other places he needed to go, and he planned to go a different way as often as possible. At Guide Dogs, they had warned the students not to get their dogs so used to familiar courses that they became routine.

"If you always walk down the same street to go to

school, what will happen when you walk down that street on a weekend and want to go to your favorite hamburger place instead? Your dog just might insist on dragging you to school because that's where he is programmed to go."

Mixing up the routes was good for Squire, and it also benefitted Mike. The more he knew, the less likely it was that he would get lost.

He probably knew the campus better than any other student. He found a popular underground utility tunnel that many used as a shortcut between two of the buildings. It meant dodging overhead pipes, but Squire quickly learned to navigate those areas and alerted Mike when it was time to duck. At night, Mike found that the tunnel was a great place to exercise Squire. He could throw a favorite toy and Squire could run to fetch it. Sometimes, the bounce of the toy would be followed by a holler or loud gasp that echoed through the tunnel.

"Sorry!" Mike shouted each time, knowing that one of his fellow students had collided with either the dog toy or Squire.

One nice thing about college was that many more of Mike's books were available in Braille or as recordings. Volunteers donated their time to record or convert the print to Braille. Back in 1968, there were no computers and only a very few extremely expensive systems for mass-producing Braille, so the process was long and tedious. While Mike could use recorded books for some of his subjects, physics and mathematics required so much review and flipping throughout the book that they needed to be in Braille in order for Mike to study them properly.

Every now and then, Mike got assigned a book that wasn't available in a form he could read, and he had to hire a reader. The readers were usually other students who wanted to make extra money and were paid by a campus rehabilitation center to read printed material out loud. Meeting with readers required extra time, which added to the stress of keeping up with his assignments.

Mike had heard that college was fun. He heard lots of talk about parties and water polo games and other events that he wished he could join in on, but during that first year, he forced himself to stay focused on his grades. Some of his teachers did a good job of describing what they wrote on the blackboard while others didn't, so those classes were much more difficult. It paid off when he made the dean's list the very first quarter and continued to. Still, it felt isolating to know that everyone else was having a good time while he sat in his dorm room studying. When he found out that some of his classmates had formed study groups but hadn't asked him to join, he couldn't help feeling left out. He would have gotten a lot out of a group like that. *Why didn't they ask me?*

He didn't need to think very long or hard about the possible reason. Deep down he knew that his blindness had something to do with it. No longer living with his family or going to a school where teachers knew him well made it all the more obvious that his inability to see made some people uncomfortable.

Will I ever feel like part of a group? Having Squire as a friend was great, but it would also be nice to have some other guys to hang out with, even if all they did was study.

♥ 🐕 ♥ 🐕 ♥

College dorm life was a new experience in itself, nothing like those weeks at Guide Dogs for the Blind or the summer he spent at UC Santa Cruz. Somehow, Mike, who was interested in all things scientific, ended up in a dormitory filled with guys from the sports teams. They were nice, but they tended to be loud and less focused on academics, as well as enjoy some very interesting forms of entertainment, like pulling pranks on one another.

One night, Mike went across the hall to go over a physics assignment with one of his classmates. He didn't need Squire to walk across the hall, so he left his dog in his dorm room.

Once they finished, Mike returned to his room, but when he opened the door, he sensed an absence.

"Squire?"

He waited for Squire to run to him. He didn't.

How did he get out? His mind suddenly flashed back to that dog on Sumac Street. Had Squire figured out how to open the door?

"Squire," Mike called. "Come."

The guy in the dorm room next to his opened his door. "Everything okay, Mike?"

"Have you seen Squire?"

"No, sorry."

"Where would he go?" Mike checked every place he could think of.

"Squire?" Mike hesitated as he poked his head into the restroom. The fact that he couldn't see wouldn't keep a guy from getting upset if his face suddenly appeared in the shower stall.

Mike's heart raced. *If Squire were hurt, I would have heard a yelp. Right?*

He didn't hear anything. He opened the shower doors. No Squire.

Mike made his way down the hall and into the main common room, where a bunch of guys from the football team were watching television.

"Have any of you seen Squire?"

"No."

"I haven't seen him since you got back from dinner."

Their voices sounded strained, like they were

trying to keep from laughing.

"This is serious," Mike told them. "I would really appreciate your help finding him."

"Come on," one of them finally said. "Let's help him out."

They disappeared for a few minutes only to return and insist, "We couldn't find him" before going back to the program they'd been watching.

Irritation mixed with Mike's concern for Squire. Couldn't they see what a big deal this was? He knocked on every door on his floor. Just when he was about to report his lost dog to anyone with authority, Eric, one of the guys from the living room, called his name.

He pulled Mike aside, keeping his voice low. "I have a confession to make. Some of us took Squire out of your room and hid him in one of the showers."

Mike wanted to yell at him. How could they do such a thing? Didn't they understand that Squire had a purpose? But this wasn't time to get confrontational. He did need Eric's help. Instead he informed him, "I checked in there."

Mike followed Eric into the restroom. "Maybe you just checked the wrong shower. Come on."

Mike called Squire's name again. This time, he heard a familiar jingle of tags and tap of toenails on tile. Squire ran to Mike, as happy as could be.

"Squire." Mike crouched down and reached for his

dog. "Where have you been?"

It was as if Squire had been in on the joke, ignoring Mike's calls until he knew his poor handler couldn't take anymore.

"If you weren't such a great dog, I would be really mad at you." He fought to restrain his anger over his dorm mates' irresponsible behavior.

Eric grew uncomfortably quiet. He paced for a moment then cleared his throat. "Listen, Mike, I'm really sorry. We were jerks. It was only meant as a joke, honest. I guess we forgot how important Squire is. I'll tell the guys to leave your dog alone after this, okay?"

Mike held Squire's collar, wanting to keep him close. "If Squire gets hurt, he can't guide anymore. I appreciate your apology, though, and thanks for the help. It really can't happen again, okay?"

"It won't. I'll tell the guys you found him."

Mike grinned. "No, wait. I have a better idea." Now that the scare was over, he was in the mood for some fun. "Let's get even."

"Great idea!"

Mike sneaked back to his room with Squire and hurried him through the door before telling Eric the rest of the plan. "Keep quiet, Squire. Don't let me down." If his dog could be in on one joke, he could be in on another.

Mike and Eric tried to look as upset as possible

when they went back to the living room.

"Hey, guys." Eric pretended to be out of breath like he'd been running all over searching. "Mike's dog isn't in the bathroom."

"What did you do with him?" Mike scowled.

"What?" One of them jumped off the couch. "You're kidding."

Every guy in the room fell silent. They hopped up and raced to the restroom.

"Where did he go?" one of them started opening shower and toilet stalls, frantically searching every corner.

The group rushed up and down the hallways, looking in dorm rooms and supply closets. While they searched, Mike and Eric tiptoed to Mike's room and moved Squire downstairs to the living room.

A few minutes later, the group thundered down the stairs.

"I don't know what to tell you. We can't find him anywhere."

Then they spotted Squire in the middle of the room. "What? But he . . ."

"So, you didn't have any idea where he was, huh?" Mike let out a laugh. "Joke's on you now."

Something about that night broke the ice between Mike and his dorm mates. They seemed to have greater respect for him. He recognized that the kidnapping plot was their way of saying they saw him as an equal—that he wasn't too helpless to handle a practical joke.

They started inviting him to join them for spontaneous activities, and they even included him in some of their pranks. The one on the receiving end always got mad, but he got over it just as Mike had.

During college, Mike found another way to be like the other guys—he bought his first car. The fact that he didn't have a license limited him quite a bit, but the campus police grew accustomed to seeing his 1964 Ford Mustang, with Mike behind the wheel and one of his sighted friends in the passenger seat.

Mike turned the steering wheel to the left, still amazed by how smooth and light a 3,000-pound car felt when he pressed his right foot to the gas pedal. He'd expected to put more effort into steering, but it glided down the road with almost as much ease as his bike. *What would the neighbors think if they saw me now? Mom and Dad would definitely be getting some angry calls.*

The next weekend, they were having a parade of cars on campus and Mike planned to drive in it. *Maybe he should invite some of his old neighbors from Palmdale to watch the festivities?*

"Brake. Brake!" His roommate Darrell's cry from the passenger seat brought Mike back to reality.

Mike slammed on the break. "What did I almost hit?"

"Just the fine arts building. Nothing important."

"I got that far off course?"

"Just joking. You were about to hit the curb in front of the fine arts building. Hang a right."

Mike slowly turned the steering wheel to the right. Soon, he was headed straight again.

"Hey, you want me to drive for a while?" Darrell sounded nervous.

"Are you kidding? This is the most fun I've had all week."

No wonder the kids at Palmdale High couldn't wait to get their driver's licenses. His Mustang had a leaky transmission that constantly needed filling, and he could only drive on campus, aided by a friend. In most cases, his friends drove while he directed them to their destination from the passenger seat, but that didn't diminish the thrill. Owning a car was the most wonderful feeling in the world.

While the campus police learned to keep an eye out for Mike's Mustang, his fellow students began listening for his voice on the campus radio station, KUCI. As a teenager, Mike had fallen in love with old radio shows from the 1930s and '40s. Every Sunday night from six to nine, Mike played those old programs on his very own radio show. Sometimes, he mixed it up a little and interviewed students or even actors from some of the old shows he played. Other nights he encouraged people to call in to discuss specific topics, or he told jokes. His radio program uncovered a hidden talent, as Mike discovered that he didn't mind expressing his opinion or talking to people he didn't know. In fact, he enjoyed it a lot. Everyone on campus knew Mike was blind, so as often as he could, he worked in jokes about his sight, hoping it would help his friends feel more comfortable to know he had a sense of humor about it. Through his radio show, he finally felt like he belonged.

Squire became as well known on the UC Irvine campus as Mike, so well known that when Mike graduated in 1972 with highest honors, Squire was presented with his own honorary degree. Mike's parents and brother applauded louder than anyone else as Mike and his aging golden retriever crossed the stage to receive their diplomas.

While other students left campus after graduation, Mike stayed to earn his master's degree in physics and a teaching credential. Besides Ellery, Mike was the first Hingson to graduate from college, and now he was going further than even he planned.

But graduate school brought a sad goodbye with it. In Mike's senior year he had noticed that Squire was moving slower and didn't see as well at night as he used to. When Mike started his first year of graduate studies he knew the time was coming when he would need to retire his best friend. He put it off as long as he could knowing it would be heartbreaking to part with the dog that had walked by his side since high school. But retirement would be better for Squire and for him. It was time to let Squire live out the remainder of his days with Mom and Dad instead of working.

In the summer of 1973, after so many years with Squire by his side, Mike entrusted Squire to his parents and went back to the Guide Dogs for the Blind campus to meet a new canine friend to travel with him into the next chapter of his life.

Part 2: Mike and Roselle Together

13

A MAN NAMED MIKE

Roselle, 1999

Roselle walked at Dave's side, down a long hallway toward the trainer's office. She could still smell the citrusy scent of shampoo on her coat from her trip to the grooming room. She'd received baths since arriving on campus, but this one felt special. The volunteers took extra care as they washed her in one of the giant tubs, moved her to a drying area that blew warm air, brushed her, and clipped and filed her nails, making her extra beautiful for Dog Day.

Roselle strutted past one of the other trainers and a new golden Lab-retriever mix guide-dog-in-training. Dave stopped in front of his office door.

Roselle could sense the presence of someone new,

someone just as excited as she was.

My person is in that room.

Dave opened the door. A big man with graying strawberry blond hair sat very still in the chair across the room. Roselle stopped. The man looked familiar. Where had she seen him before?

"Mike, meet Roselle."

Mike. I like that name.

Roselle studied Mike more closely. His hands rested on his knees, his fingers twitching like he wanted very badly to reach out but needed to stay still. He was nervous; she could feel the tension in his body from across the room. But he also seemed to know what to expect. He seemed . . . confident. Then Roselle remembered.

Yesterday! Mike was the man I saw talking on the bench.

She walked right over and sniffed Mike's hand then his pants and shirt. He smelled like a nice man. Mike remained still until the trainer gave him the go-ahead to move, then he immediately reached for Roselle and gently stroked her head and face. She looked up at him. He smiled.

"Hello, Roselle." His voice was strong.

She gave him her sweetest doggy smile. Hello, Mike.

"Well," he rubbed her ears and patted her back. "I think I found a friend."

I think I did too. He had a friendly, intelligent face. He looked like a man who would take her for a lot of exciting adventures.

"Roselle definitely has the on/off switch you asked for, Mike," Dave said.

She looked at Mike then at the trainer. *What is an on/off switch?* No one had mentioned her having one before.

"When Roselle is working, she is all business, but when that harness comes off, she will run and play and steal your socks like any ordinary dog. According to her puppy raisers, you might want to keep your slippers under lock and key."

Mike cupped Roselle's face in his hands. "So, you're a thief, huh?"

It had been months since Roselle stole Kay's slippers. She'd never considered stealing socks, but now that Dave mentioned it, those might be even better. *Socks will be a lot easier to hide in my mouth while sneaking down the hall.*

"Karen and I better keep an eye on the valuables." Mike laughed and patted Roselle's back. "I guess we should head back to our room so the next student can come in. Roselle, come."

Roselle felt two tails taller as she left Dave's office with Mike. Unless they had trouble connecting and needed to be reassigned, she and Mike would spend every moment of their remaining weeks on campus together.

That evening at dinner, Roselle sat at Mike's feet, staring at the other dogs through the table legs and people feet. While listening in to their mealtime conversations, she learned that Mike's full name was Michael Hingson and that Karen was Mike's wife. He and the other students were part of a three-week course that Guide Dogs for the Blind had started offering for those who could not be away from home or work for the longer four-week class. Mike and Karen lived in New Jersey. Karen had once worked as a special education teacher then became a travel agent, specializing in making travel easier for people with disabilities. Mike worked for a computer company called Quantum/ATL. The company provided data protection and network storage systems. Mike was a regional sales manager. Roselle had no idea what data protection or network storage were or what a regional sales manager did, but Mike's classmates seemed impressed so she figured it must be important. He commuted to New York City to work in a place called The World Trade Center.

Roselle's ears perked up the first time Mike mentioned New York. *I've been there!*

"I hope Roselle likes subway trains and cabs," Mike told the man beside him, "because she will be spending a lot of time in them."

The subway. I've been there too. Her ears drooped

a bit. But cab drivers don't like me. I guess he'll find out soon enough.

After dinner, Mike and his friends relaxed in the common room. A lady played some songs on the piano and a few others gathered around her to sing. Roselle rested from her exciting day while Mike and his friends talked, read Braille books, chatted on their cell phones, and used the computers. Some of the computers read all the text from the screen out loud, so the listener had to put headphones on; others magnified it so large that Roselle could see the letters and images from across the room. One man sat in front of a screen that had a tray underneath it, where he placed a book. The words popped up on the screen and he moved a knob until the words were large enough for him to read. Roselle finally fell asleep watching a lady wind string around two long sticks to make something that looked like part of a sock. So that is how socks are made.

Roselle spent the night in Mike's dorm room. She met Mike's roommate, a young college-aged man named Adam. At bedtime, Mike tethered her to a short cable near a special sleep area beside his bed. Adam did the same with his dog. If either of them needed their dogs in the middle of the night, they would know exactly where to find them.

The next morning, Roselle began training with Mike. They started with a daily obedience exercise.

Mike and the other students gave simple commands while the trainers evaluated each team's progress and performance.

"Heel," Mike said.

Roselle went around to Mike's left side and sat. She had done this hundreds of times for Todd, but she needed to prove her ability to obey her handler.

"Good girl. Now, down."

Roselle dropped to her belly.

"Good!" Mike grinned at Roselle. "Sit."

Roselle hopped up and sat without moving from her spot beside Mike. She looked up at him. *This is fun, and Mike is really good at it.*

Mike took her through the same routine three times in a row then he began to walk away. He held his hand out. "Stay."

She stayed put as Mike walked to the end of the leash then returned to his place beside her. He walked away again, but this time he called to her, "Come."

Roselle bounded up and went to Mike as quickly as she could. Mike knelt in front of her. "Good girl, Roselle!" He smothered her with strokes and praise. "They sure gave me a great dog."

♥ 🐕 ♥ 🐕 ♥

For their first training session they took a walk around San Rafael. Roselle was a pretty fast walker, but so was Mike. As they weaved in and out of crowds, crossed streets, and did all the things the trainers asked them to do, Mike constantly praised Roselle.

"You're going to do a great job in New York City crowds, Roselle." Mike stroked her head.

One of the first things that Roselle noticed when she started working with Mike was his habit of making a clicking sound with his tongue. He said it was his way of hearing his surroundings, and it seemed to help him find things like steps, curbs, trees, and doorways. The clicking didn't bother her. Many of the students at Guide Dogs for the Blind had unique methods for getting around and finding things that they couldn't see.

Roselle discovered immediately that Mike knew what he was doing. He was quick to encourage the other students and offer pointers. When his roommate Adam commented on it during a walk around campus, Roselle discovered how much experience Mike had.

"Roselle is my fifth guide dog," Mike said.

"Fifth? How long have you been working with dogs?"

"I was a few years younger than you when I got my first, Squire. After retiring him, I got Holland. IIc was a big goof off. He enjoyed walking me into mailboxes. Next there was Klondike, then Linnie. Linnie was probably my favorite so far. She was a great guide and wonderful with people. Unfortunately, she contracted Lyme disease from a tick bite last year and had to retire. Karen and I kept her as a pet. It'll be interesting to see how she and Roselle get along."

Adam directed his dog to the left. "I still feel clueless."

"You won't feel clueless forever."

"I was so excited when I got my dog, and really nervous. I guess it was no big deal to you, considering how many times you've gone through Dog Day."

"You would be surprised. Receiving a new dog never stops being exciting, and I am always nervous. I have gone six months without a dog. After Linnie got sick, I traveled with a cane for a while, but I got tired of replacing them. New Yorkers are usually in too much of a hurry to watch where they're going, so I had more canes stepped on and broken than I can count. I could hardly wait to get a dog again. But as always, I sat in Dave's office wondering if Roselle and I would be a good match. Despite her criminal tendencies, we definitely are. It takes time to build the relationship, so be patient with yourself."

"So far, we get along great. I'm just not used to a dog leading me around, you know."

"Remember, he isn't leading you around; it's a partnership. You and your dog are a team."

The words partnership and team echoed in Roselle's ears. Instead of it being all up to her to keep

Mike safe and headed in the right direction, they would work together.

After a week of daily walks and classes, they finally had their first Sunday off. That day, Mike took some time out to read in his room. Roselle snoozed beside his bed. She woke up to the sound of him fighting to hold back laughter. Her head shot up. What am I missing?

"Roselle, you snore!" He finally let out the howl he'd been repressing.

She dropped her head back down. What was it with these claims that she snored? First the Sterns, then Todd, and now Mike. She didn't hear a thing.

❤ 🐕 ❤ 🐕 ❤

The next week, Roselle's work with Mike changed. Instead of joining the rest of the group in San Rafael, she and Mike traveled to San Francisco. It turned out that Mike had a busy work schedule to get back to in New York and could not stay for the entire three-week session. With so much experience under his belt, the trainers made some special arrangements for the new team to practice in crowded areas, as well as riding public transportation, escalators, and taxis. Mike did these things every day as part of his work routine, now he had to do them with Roselle. Leading Mike through busy office buildings, the BART train station, and streets packed with businessmen and women felt overwhelming at first. People rushed and shoved and didn't watch where they were going. Streetlights didn't seem to matter to some drivers, forcing Roselle to work twice as hard to keep Mike safe. But Mike praised her constantly, even on days when she needed extra help and guidance.

"You're going to do fine in New York, Roselle."

Roselle returned from her trips to San Francisco exhausted and ready to crash beside Mike's bed. She awoke ready for action the next day. As Mike prepared to get dressed, Roselle saw him lay something white on the foot of his bed. It immediately rolled off. She was still tethered, but the rope was just long enough for her to reach Mike's bed. She padded over for a look and a sniff.

Socks! Clean and bright and just sitting there on the floor. She glanced at Mike, who was in front of the closet running his fingers over Braille labels in his shirts until he found the one he wanted. Once he selected one, he went to the shower without turning back for his socks. Roselle nudged them with her nose. Adam's dog snoozed beside his handler's desk while Adam read a Braille book. The socks smelled so fresh. She touched them with her nose again. They are so soft.

Roselle snatched up the socks. It felt just like old times, except she didn't have the Stern's house to run around to find a good hiding place. Tail wagging,

Roselle returned to her sleeping place, the socks turning into a damp wad in her mouth. She heard the water in the shower turn off. A few minutes later, Mike returned.

"I know I took out a pair of socks." He touched the top of his dresser then went to his bed and ran his hands over it. "Where did they go?"

Roselle curled up a little tighter. Her tags clinked. Mike immediately turned.

"Roselle, what are you up to?"

Adam put his book down. "I think she's hiding."

"Roselle." Mike's voice sounded playfully stern. "Come."

She popped her head up. Mike leaned down and ran his hands over her face. His hands stopped at her bulging jaws.

"What's in your mouth?" He tugged the end hanging out of Roselle's mouth. "Wait, are those my socks?"

Roselle let them drop into Mike hands. Mike's face scrunched in disgust.

"Eww, they're all wet."

Adam laughed. "Ah, man, that's nasty."

Roselle waited for Mike to laugh along with Adam. His mouth clearly wanted to smile, but he forced it to stay serious. He shook the moist ball. "Stealing socks is not a good thing, Roselle."

Roselle's ears dropped. She said sorry with her

eyes. He dropped the soppy socks in his laundry bag and took another pair out of his drawer.

"Come, Roselle. Time to start our day."

Roselle and Mike sailed through their daily activities together. On December 4, Mike and Roselle left Guide Dogs for the Blind for their return trip to New Jersey.

"You're going to miss graduation." Adam sat on the edge of his bed as Roselle followed Mike around the dorm room, watching him pack.

"I know." Roselle detected sadness in Mike's voice. "I hate missing it, and this means the Sterns won't be able to present me with Roselle, but I couldn't get away for the full three weeks."

Roselle stopped. *I'll miss seeing Ted and Kay?*

"I'm anxious to get back and introduce her to Karen and Linnie though, and of course the cats. Cali and Sherlock might not be too happy with a second dog to deal with, but they'll all learn to get along or leave each other alone eventually."

Cats? I can deal with them. Cats often wandered onto campus, so she had plenty of experience with their it's-all-about-me attitudes.

"And the sooner I get her accustomed to my routine the better."

Right after breakfast, Roselle climbed into one of the school vans with Mike and said goodbye to Guide Dogs for the Blind. One of the trainers drove them to the San Francisco airport. Roselle walked proudly at Mike's side. Instead of entering the airport as a puppy-in-training, she was walking in as a guide dog, officially working for Mike and able to board the plane without question. She watched him pick up his ticket and check his suitcase at baggage claim like any other passenger, then they walked to his assigned gate. The trainer stayed with them, but Mike didn't need any help from him. He stood in line, got his boarding pass, and found a place in the waiting area with everyone else, only stopping to ask questions about things he couldn't see, like signs.

Roselle waited at Mike's feet until a voice came over the loudspeaker announcing their flight.

"That's us." Mike said goodbye to the trainer and shook his hand. Roselle watched the man walk away to head back to campus and train other dogs.

They followed the line of people heading toward the airplane. Roselle kept a close eye on the rolling suitcases, changes in the walkway, and passengers who weren't watching out for others.

As soon as they boarded the plane, Mike stopped. "Roselle, do you want to meet someone?"

He dropped her harness and told her to go left. Mike's direction led her to a tiny room filled with buttons and screens and instruments. Two men in uniforms sat in chairs facing the screens. When they swiveled around, but men jolted back in their seats.

Then one of them laughed and the other man grinned.

"Well, hello pooch." One of the pilots got up and patted Roselle's back.

Mike stood at the door. "Roselle thought she'd introduce herself before we take off."

A lady who wore a navy blue and white uniform and looked like she also did something important poked her head into the cockpit. "Excuse me, sir, what is going on?"

The pilot answered for Mike. "Just a furry passenger making friends."

The other pilot assured her, "We're fine."

"Why don't you say hello to the flight attendant too, Roselle?" Mike stepped aside and Roselle greeted the lady in the uniform by kissing her hand with her nose.

She reached down to pet Roselle between the ears. Her hands were a little stiff, like she didn't know how she felt about having a dog on her flight. "Nice to meet you. I, um . . . look forward to serving you, today. Can I show you two to your seat?"

Mike picked up Roselle's harness. "That would be lovely. Thank you."

When Mike and Roselle arrived at their seat, he released the harness handle and turned Roselle, forcing her to back into their row. When she flew with the Sterns, she had no problem finding a spot to curl up under Kay's seat, but now she could barely get in. Had she really grown so much or had airplanes shrunk in the last year?

"Sorry. It's a tight fit, I know." She kept backing up until Mike told her to stop. "Sit. Down. Good girl."

By the time Mike took his place in the window seat, Roselle was wedged between the side of the plane and the seats. Mike reached down and physically turned her so her bottom was under the seat in front of his. Her head stuck out between Mike's feet. She could hardly move.

"Poor thing." The lady sitting beside Mike gazed down at Roselle.

"I know it looks uncomfortable, but that is actually the safest place for her. If we hit turbulence, she will be protected."

"I never thought of that. What a great idea."

Since she couldn't move, all Roselle could do was settle in for a nap.

An hour or so later, Roselle woke up. Mike was talking to the man across the aisle.

"Do you have a dog down there? I just saw the side of its head."

"I do. This is Roselle, my new guide dog."

Roselle tried to pop her head up to say hello but hit it on the seat instead. *Ouch!*

"I didn't notice her until now."

"You hear that, Roselle? This man just paid you a

high compliment. You are doing so well that he didn't even know you were here. Keep up the good work, girl."

14

HIS EYES, HER FEET

Mike, 1999-2000

Aspecial car service drove Mike and Roselle home to New Jersey when they landed in New York that evening. After two weeks away from Karen, Mike couldn't wait to see his sweet wife. At the same time, he fought anxiety as he always did before bringing a new guide dog home. Would Roselle get along with Linnie, who was used to being top dog? Would he spend the next week listening to Cali and Sherlock hissing and Roselle yelping because she hadn't heeded the "You get any closer and the claws come out" warnings?

What will Roselle do when Karen comes out to meet us in her wheelchair?

He had known and loved Karen for so long that he hardly noticed the wheelchair anymore, just like she hardly noticed that Mike couldn't see. Everyone who knew Karen ignored the wheelchair too, but dogs, like some humans, could be mysterious creatures.

Like Mike, Karen had lived with her disability since birth and been treated no differently than her siblings. She excelled in school, went to college, became a teacher, and even drove with the help of special hand controls, which replaced the use of the foot pedals. While most people pushed the gas pedal with their foot, Karen pulled down on a lever with her left hand. To stop or slow down her car, Karen pushed forward on the same lever.

Karen had worked as a teacher for 10 years before falling in love with travel. She opened her own business focusing on making travel possible or less difficult for those living with physical handicaps, blindness, and other disabilities. In the late 1970s and into the 1980s most people still thought that those with disabilities couldn't travel on their own or at all. Airlines, car rental companies, and cruise ships lacked many accommodations for disabled travelers, such as flat entryways for wheelchairs and wide doorways.

Karen's goal was to make sure her customers had a good and exciting travel experience and got the help they needed. Karen was a true pioneer in the travel industry, but long before Mike brought Roselle home, she had retired.

In addition to travel, Karen loved quilting, so she traded her travel business for a home quilting business called Quilt Elegance.

Mike had met Karen in Southern California while having dinner with friends. Mike worked for a company that required him to go out of town often, and Karen had just started working as a travel agent. They got to know each other better when Karen started handling Mike's business trips, but what Mike really wanted was to ask Karen out on a date. He called her every day for about two months before they finally went out. They loved going to dinner and movies, where Karen described the action on the screen to Mike, but most of all they enjoyed just being together. They could talk for hours about anything and felt completely comfortable with each other. They just fit.

Learning to deal with each other's very different physical challenges could be awkward at times. Mike had to learn how to push a wheelchair, and Karen learned to trust him. At first, Karen steered as Mike pushed. They became a pretty good team. It felt nice to have this kind of partnership with a person instead of a dog. On the flip side, there were times that Mike had to read printed material for work. He didn't want Karen to feel obligated to read to him, but she seemed eager to be his eyes. These things only deepened their appreciation for the fact that each of them understood what it felt like to need help, adapt to a world designed for those who could see and walk without assistance, grow up feeling different, and be treated differently.

In early July of 1982, Mike went to a convention of the National Federation of the Blind. When he returned to Southern California, he got sick. Karen insisted that he stay with her and her parents until he was better. He remained at her home for two weeks.

At the end of his stay, Mike and Karen went out to eat. On the drive home, Mike blurted out, "What do you think of the idea of us getting married?"

"It's hard to say what I think when you haven't even proposed yet."

Mike fidgeted with his seatbelt, searching for a good recovery.

Karen stopped at an intersection.

"Well." Mike cleared his throat. "Will you marry me?"

Karen laughed. "That wasn't exactly the proposal I dreamed of as a girl, but yes, Mike. I accept."

As thrilled as he was over Karen's answer, her silent disappointment tugged at his heart. He would need to do better than a traffic stop proposal.

A few days later, he came up with a much more romantic plan that Karen could brag about to her friends. In the middle of the afternoon, he showed up at the travel agency where Karen worked. Karen was on the phone with a customer when he walked in. Karen's boss knew Mike was coming and was part of the plan for what happened next.

Mike went straight to Karen's desk. He reached into his pocket for a diamond ring he had just purchased. He felt for Karen's left hand while she was still on the phone.

His heart felt like it might explode in his chest, feeling all eyes in the office on him.

With Karen still engrossed in her phone call, Mike slipped the ring onto her finger. "Will you marry me?"

She gasped. "Um, I'm going to have to call you back. My boyfriend just proposed." She hung up without another word as the whole office erupted with applause. Work came to a halt for the next half hour so everyone could celebrate with champagne and a cake that Karen's boss had smuggled in earlier in the day.

To celebrate their engagement, Mike took Karen to a restaurant called El Tamara in Northern California. It was built into the side of a mountain and required a climb up 159 steps. Mike and Karen dated before the days of mandatory wheelchair access, and Mike was determined to take her where he knew she wanted to go. He grabbed the handles of Karen's chair and rolled her up every step to the top, letting his feet guide him as the backs of his heels hit each step. It

177

was the craziest thing he ever did for a girl.

They were married on November 27, 1982, Mike wearing a white tuxedo, Karen in a white gown and hat, with the sanctuary decorated in a beautiful combination of fall colors and peachy-pink. Mike waited at the altar with his guide dog Holland as Karen's father pushed her wheelchair down the aisle. Mom, Dad, and Ellery were there, and so was Mr. Herbo. Two ministers performed the ceremony because Karen was close to both and wanted them to be a part of her special day. After they exchanged vows, Mike took the handles of the wheelchair and escorted his radiant bride out of the church and into their new life together.

Eighteen years later, they still adored each other. Mike's mom and dad had both passed away, but he was thankful that they got to see him fall in love and marry such an incredible woman.

As nervous as he was about bringing Roselle home, Mike couldn't wait to introduce his new dog to his best friend, Karen.

It was evening when the car turned down Mike's street. He called Karen on his cell phone.

"We're almost home. Are you ready?"

"Welcome home. I'll be in the garage with Linnie, waiting for you. I'll keep the door open."

Roselle's head popped up when the car pulled into the driveway.

"We're home, girl. Ready to meet the family?"

He assumed her excited breaths meant yes. Mike paid the driver and got his luggage out of the back. Roselle stood at his side. He could feel her staring straight ahead toward the garage. What was she thinking? She probably saw Linnie and wanted to play.

"Come, Roselle." Mike headed for the garage and walked right to Karen. He bent down and kissed her. "Hello, Sweetheart. I've missed you."

"Two weeks is a long time." Karen squeezed his hard. "I see you brought home a new addition to the family."

Mike found the button for the automatic garage door and closed it. "I did." He let go of her harness but kept a firm grip on the leash. "Roselle, meet my lovely wife, Karen."

Roselle slowly made her way over to Karen. She sniffed the wheels on her chair before moving her nose to Karen's hands.

"I like to say that Karen is my eyes and I'm her feet."

Karen chuckled. "Nice to meet you, Roselle. You're a pretty one."

Linnie backed up behind Karen's wheelchair. Who is that? Roselle immediately turned her attention to the other dog.

Mike breathed out his relief. Roselle didn't seem

bothered by the wheelchair at all. She seemed more interested in Linnie than in Karen.

"Go ahead and release Linnie," Mike told his wife. "Let them get to know each other."

Mike called the dogs to follow him and Karen inside. As he and his wife caught up and talked about his trip, Mike listened in on Roselle and Linnie. After a few moments of sniffs, each dog had gone her separate way. What was that all about? Usually sniffing would be followed by play. Roselle introduced herself to Cali, who ran for the top of the refrigerator, and Sherlock the black Halloween cat, who hid under Mike and Karen's bed. When the fun was over, she sauntered back into the living room and stood beside them. Mike heard Linnie's breathing behind the couch.

"I bet they'll be chasing each other across the house by morning," Karen said.

"I hope so." It was nice that the dogs weren't fighting, but total indifference wasn't a good sign either. Mike wanted his dogs to enjoy each other's company the way Squire and Peewee and some of his other past dogs did.

Karen rode a special elevator to the second floor of their house. Mike called Roselle and Linnie to follow him up the stairs. They slept tethered to their assigned areas in the bedroom, each acting as if the other didn't exist.

♥ 🐕 ♥ 🐕 ♥

"Okay, Karen, it's time to break the ice." By mid-
afternoon on Sunday, Mike had had enough of
Roselle's and Linnie's silence and avoidance. "Watch
this."

He felt his way through Linnie's toy basket until
he found her Booda Bone—a tug toy made of rope
with a knot on each end. He held it out to Roselle.
She immediately jumped up from her spot under the
coffee table and grabbed one end, tugging with all
her strength. Linnie popped her head up, eyeing the
scene from the corner of the room like "Hey, that's
my toy."

"Oh," Karen wheeled herself closer. "I think
Linnie's getting jealous."

"Well, come join the fun." Mike slapped his knee.

Linnie scurried over. After a moment of hesitation,
she took it and Mike grabbed the middle. It wasn't
long before both dogs relaxed and declared a game of
two against one.

"Oh, now, that's not fair. I can't keep up with you
powerful beasts." He dropped his section and sat back
while Roselle and Linnie yanked and growled away.

From that moment on, Roselle and Linnie were
inseparable, bound by their mutual love of tug toys.

Later that night, Mike was working in his home
office, which was set up in the basement, when he
heard Roselle and Linnie tugging the Booda Bone

back and forth. He swiveled his chair around and rolled across the basement floor. He grabbed the middle of the rope bone.

He tugged, but he was no match for two full-grown Labs. He picked up his feet and let the two of them pull him across the room. Roselle seemed extra excited about this game. "Roselle, have you done this before?"

Their playful growls almost sounded like laughter, especially when Mike forgot about the pole in the middle of the basement connecting the ceiling and the floor, and the dogs pulled him right into it. After he recovered from the shock of the collision, Mike rubbed his head, picturing Roselle and Linnie high-fiving each other.

"You two did that on purpose."

Pull Mike into the Pole became the dogs' favorite game.

On Monday, Mike started Roselle on her new routine of riding with him to his office at the World Trade Center. It would take a while for her to learn the layout of the massive tower where he worked and get familiar with the route to and from New York, but Mike knew it was best to dive right in. Every free moment he had during the day would be dedicated to teaching Roselle every inch of his workplace just like he had when he first started working for Quantum and was traveling with his white cane.

After relieving Roselle, eating breakfast, and saying goodbye to Karen and Linnie, Mike strapped on Roselle's harness and leash and went out to meet the driver from the Happy Fox Taxi.

"Charlie," Mike told the driver as he and Roselle got settled in the backseat, "this is Roselle, my new traveling companion."

"Keep Mike under control back there, Roselle, will ya?"

Roselle rested her head on Mike's feet as the taxi took them to the New Jersey Transit Station, where they would board a commuter train to New York City. Roselle didn't seem to notice the bustle of the station. When their train arrived, she hopped right on like she'd been riding it all her life.

In Newark, Mike and Roselle transferred to the PATH train that went straight to the World Trade Center and ran between the two 110-story towers, dropping them off in an underground concourse. The concourse felt like a city in itself, buzzing with activity and people. There were restaurants and shops, all part of the incredible structures known as the Twin Towers. The North Tower had opened in December 1970; the South Tower debuted in 1972. Now, the World Trade Center was a focal point of the New York City landscape.

Mike directed Roselle toward the elevator for Tower One, the North Tower. On the ride up, Mike proudly introduced his new friend to everyone who entered the elevator.

They got off at the 78th floor and Mike directed Roselle down the hall to room 7827, home of Quantum/ATL.

"Here we are. My home away from home."

Mike's office was more of a suite, consisting of four large rooms. One room was Mike's personal office where he kept his computer with special software that spoke aloud whatever text came across the screen. He also had a special printer for Braille. Mike's office was to the left of the reception and demo room. A conference room was to the right of that, and farther right was the office where the sales people worked. When Mike wanted to show presentations, he would bring his computer into the conference room rather than having a second special computer there. Although he was thankful for this new technology, he still treasured the first Braillewriter that his parents ordered from Germany so many years ago. He had it proudly displayed in his office. Clients and visitors often commented on the strange-looking machine, allowing Mike to share stories about his incredible parents and their refusal to let a little thing like blindness hold him back.

Roselle settled right into the routine of the office.

It wasn't long before Roselle assigned herself the job of office greeter. Whenever the outer door opened Roselle jumped up, even from a sound sleep, to beat everyone else to the door and meet the new arrival. Welcome! Welcome! I'm so glad you're here.

The Christmas season was a blur as Mike and Roselle worked on developing their partnership and Roselle adjusted to life with the Hingsons. At home, Linnie was Roselle's best buddy. It wasn't long before she felt comfortable enough with Cali and Sherlock to tease them, resulting in a few scratches. By spring, Roselle had settled into her daily routine of accompanying Mike to The World Trade Center. On weekends, she went with Mike and Karen to church, shows, or to visit friends. She sat in her place on the backseat while Karen drove and Mike acted as navigator.

One afternoon in May, Mike was at work when he received a phone call from a woman whose name he had heard during his training with Roselle.

"Mike? It's Kay Stern. I know we've never met, but my husband Ted and I raised Roselle as a puppy."

"Oh yes, Kay. Hello."

Roselle immediately perked up.

The Sterns were in New York and wanted to visit. Kay and Ted came right over to the World Trade Center to meet Mike and see Roselle.

Before they arrived Mike called Karen. "How

would you like to have company for dinner? The Sterns are in town."

"The Sterns? Of course, please invite them over."

Kay and Ted arrived at the World Trade Center in time for lunch.

"Roselle! Look at you." Kay crouched down as Roselle ran right over. She threw her arms around Roselle's neck. "I've missed you."

Roselle kissed Kay's nose.

"Well, don't you look official?" Ted rubbed Roselle's head.

Mike enjoyed being part of the reunion and finally having the chance to meet the couple that raised such a remarkable dog.

15

THE STORM

Roselle, September 11, 2001

I n the year and a half since Roselle joined Mike and Karen, she and Mike had become quite a team. She loved living in their house in New Jersey and going to work each day at the World Trade Center. The cab drivers not only let her ride, but they greeted her like a friend. There was only one thing that Roselle didn't enjoy about living in New Jersey: the thunderstorms. She had never experienced them while living with the Sterns in Santa Barbara or at the Guide Dogs campus in San Rafael. *What is wrong with New Jersey?*

"It took me a while to get used to the thunder," Mike said one night as Roselle trembled and whined.

She leaned her head against his knee, dreaded each flash of light, knowing a loud boom would follow within seconds, sounding like the sky might split down the middle. *What if it does? Can the sky do that?*

"Pretty soon, you'll sleep right through them."

She never did.

Just after midnight on September 11, 2001, Roselle awoke to the wind rattling the windows. A storm was coming; she could feel it in the air. She shook on her blanket beside Mike and Karen's bed. Her attempts not to whimper only made her quiver more violently. She heard Mike roll over in bed. He reached down and stroked her back, then her ears. Even the feel of Mike's strong hand didn't erase the terror.

She nosed his hand. Mike, *I'm scared.*

"Your nose is so warm. You need to calm down. Shh. It's only wind."

Only wind? How can you say that? You know the thunder is coming any minute. She panted harder and louder.

He sat up and pulled back the covers.

"Come on." Mike said through a yawn. "I don't want you to wake Karen. If you're going to keep me up half the night, I might as well get some work done."

He rubbed Roselle's chin and neck then stuck his feet into the slippers beside his bed. Roselle nuzzled his legs. *Thank you, Mike. Thank for not making me face this frightening night alone.*

Roselle's nails tapped the oak floor as she followed

Mike down the hall then down the stairs to the first floor of the house, past the door to Karen's elevator, and down another set of steps to Mike's home office. The first rolls of thunder began to rumble before they reached the last step. Roselle's paws had barely touched the basement floor before she dove for safety under Mike's desk.

"Looking at you right now, one would never guess that I put my life in your hands every day of the week." Mike turned on the radio to a news program, drowning out the booms outside.

Roselle curled up into a cocoon at Mike's feet. I'm not coming out until it's over!

"I guess I could use the extra time to prepare for my big presentation this morning."

Once Mike booted up his computer, Roselle took comfort in the rhythmic tap of the keys and the gentle murmur of the screen reader—a program that read every word that Mike typed or needed to read. The screen reader read in a low monotone voice that calmed Roselle's racing heart.

It wasn't long before the thunder grew too loud to be covered by the sound of Mike's radio and computer. The storm settled right over his house. Roselle trembled and no longer tried to hold back her pitiful whining. Nothing Mike did could relax her.

"Wow." Mike straightened up in his chair as a loud boom shook the house. "It sounds like bombs going off."

Roselle shook even harder. *Bombs. That didn't sound like a good word.*

But an hour and a half later, the storm had moved on, Roselle had slowly relaxed under Mike's pats and reassuring words, and the Hingson house returned to its usual nighttime calm. She had almost fallen back to sleep when Mike pushed his chair back and gently nudged her. "Roselle, come. I still have time to get a few hours of sleep. I have a big day."

Roselle stretched her way out from under the desk and followed Mike back to the bedroom. She could make up for the lost sleep during Mike's meeting.

She awoke to the buzz of Mike's shaver. Karen was still asleep.

Roselle scratched the back of her neck and looked pathetically out the window. That was the worst night ever.

But as soon as Mike emerged from the bathroom, Roselle began tracking his every move. Mike turned on the television as he ate his favorite cereal, Special K, and drank his tea. From the sound of the news, something important was going on. In a few hours, New York would elect a new mayor.

Mike rinsed out his bowl then went back upstairs to say goodbye to Karen. Roselle followed him.

"I'll save you a ham and cheese croissant," he whispered before kissing her on the cheek.

"There won't be any left, you know that."

"Well, I'll think of something else to bring you then."

"Thanks." Karen yawned. "See you tonight."

"Love you." Mike kissed her again.

Mike grabbed Roselle's harness and leash off the hook beside the front door and called for her. As usual, Roselle sprang into action. Time for work.

Charlie, the cab driver from Happy Fox Taxi, picked them up at the curb and drove them to the New Jersey Transit Station. They arrived in plenty of time to catch their train, only to find out it would be delayed by 15 minutes.

"Great," Mike groaned. "Of all the days. So much for getting to work early."

They barely made the PATH train to the World Trade Center.

As soon as they stepped off the train, Mike and Roselle headed to the elevator. They got off at the 78th floor and Mike reached into his suit pocket for keys to room 7827. The breakfast that Mike had ordered for the meeting arrived seconds later. Roselle smelled the heavenly ham and cheese croissants that Mike always referred to as "the best in the world."

If I could only taste one and judge for myself.

Mike removed Roselle's harness and helped set up for breakfast. Next to arrive was David Frank, a man from the Quantum office in California who was in

New York for the meeting. Six people arrived with him, and Roselle immediately stepped into her role of greeter.

"Morning, Roselle." David stroked Roselle's neck. He was tall and quiet, quite different from Mike who loved to talk.

"What a beautiful Lab," one of the women who'd arrived with Dave said. "Is it okay to pet her?"

"Sure," Mike told her. "Roselle is on her coffee break right now."

Mike and David directed everyone to the conference room. With no new people to greet or get attention from, Roselle found her favorite spot under Mike's desk and snuggled her head on his feet, the best pillow in the world. She loved being able to feel his every movement. She drifted off to the sound of Mike and David going over the details of their presentation on Mike's laptop.

When Mike carefully slipped his feet out from under her head, Roselle barely felt it. Then, came a violent jolt.

What a strange dream.

Roselle opened her eyes.

She heard a loud boom and felt the building swaying sideways. She could hear screams from the conference room and Mike and David calling out,

"What was that?"

"An earthquake maybe?"

"No, it doesn't feel like one."

"Do you think there was an explosion somewhere?"

"Would we feel it all the way up here?

"The building feels like it's falling over."

"God," Mike whispered. "Don't let this building tip over."

Then Mike and David were saying goodbye to each other, and they both sounded like they were about to cry.

Is this a dream? It feels so real.

Roselle yawned. She stretched her neck out from under the desk. Then she saw Mike. He was standing in the doorway, holding onto the frame for dear life. He looked confused. No, it was another kind of look, something she wasn't used to seeing on his face. Fear.

The building was still swaying to one side.

Then slowly, the building straightened up again.

Roselle crawled out from under the desk and looked around? What just happened?

Papers, books, tiles from the ceiling, and pieces of building material cluttered the floor.

Whatever had happened, Roselle felt strangely calm. Mike let go of the doorframe, hurried over, and felt for her leash.

David looked out the window behind Mike's desk. "Oh no!"

"What is it?" Mike joined David at the window.

"Outside, there is smoke . . . fire . . . papers and debris flying everywhere. I see glass, like the windows above us were blown out."

Roselle could hear it now. Through the window, she saw a storm like none she had ever experienced. Far worse than last night's thunder. Shards of glass tapped the window like hail. A piece of paper smacked against the window then flew away again.

"God, help," someone cried from the conference room.

"Where's the emergency exit?"

Roselle stood erect but calm. *Get ready to focus.*

David stood by the front window. Black smoke billowed. "We have to get out of here, now!"

16

1,463 STAIRS

Mike

Mike clutched Roselle's leash. The screaming from the room next door had turned to frightened, desperate sobs. Through it all, Roselle seemed completely at ease. If she wasn't panicking, everything must be okay.

David's words echoed in his ears. We have to get out of here, now!

"I agree," Mike told his friend. "But let's slow down and do it the right way, okay?"

They had fire drills in the Tower every six months, so he knew the rules: avoid the elevator, use the stairs, and don't panic. He had spent his first weeks at Quantum learning every inch of Tower One, so he wasn't worried about finding his way out.

"We need to show our guests to the exit first. Get

them to a stairwell and then come back here. When you get back we will leave."

David obeyed.

Karen. She needs to know I'm okay before this hits the news.

He picked up his desk phone and dialed his home phone number. The sound of his wife's voice calmed his spirit.

"Listen, Honey, there has been some kind of explosion. We're okay, but we're leaving the building now."

"Mike, are you sure you're okay?" Her usually gentle tone was edged with anxiety.

"Don't worry, David and Roselle and I are together. I'll call again as soon as I can."

Beside him, Roselle was still as relaxed as ever.

David returned right after Mike hung up.

"We better shut the computers down." David sat, sneaking an anxious glance toward the window.

Mike and David got to work saving their files and shutting down laptops, until David said, "This is taking too long. We need to get out."

"You're right. Let's go." He grabbed his briefcase and his phone, then strapped Roselle into her harness. She wagged her tail and looked up, ready to do her job.

David swung his laptop case over his shoulder and opened the door.

"Forward," Mike said to Roselle.

Mike and Roselle moved through the doorway and out into the glass-and-debris-covered hallway. Even as tiles and plaster fell from the ceiling and people rushed for the exit, Roselle kept moving ahead. Mike directed her to Stairwell B, which meant going through an area of the building known as the sky lobby. He knew exactly where it was—in the center of the lobby, between the two elevators. The voices around him revealed nothing about what happened, but their intensity and the smoke around him sped up his pace. Something was wrong; that was all he needed to know.

Mike instructed Roselle forward again when they reached the top of the stairs.

What are we getting ourselves into? He grabbed the metal handrail, wondering how many other people were already on the stairs ahead of him, Roselle, and David. *How long will it take us to get down?*

Roselle's calmness settled Mike's nerves. She was relaxed and ready to do her job of watching for people and any possible hazards ahead.

Around him, people were surprisingly calm and quiet, caring only about getting out. The stairwell wasn't nearly as crowded as expected. But it was a long way down, and Mike knew it. Each of the 78 floors had two short flights—first ten stairs, then a

180-degree turn, then nine more stairs. Mike did the math in his head.

That was 1,463 stairs.

As Roselle and Mike began the long descent, Mike's senses went on high alert. He hadn't heard any more explosions since that one in the office. No fire alarms had gone off; no announcement over the PA system offering information or instructions. Why the silence? With no cell phone signals available in the cave-like stairwell, none of them could call family members or receive calls with news of what was going on. Their whole world consisted of stairs and concrete walls and the question of what they would find when they reached the bottom. How long would it be before they could return to their offices? He still had a presentation to give.

The unknown felt like torture. When it got to be too much, Mike listened to Roselle. She was focusing intensely. Her panting grew heavier.

"That smell," a man behind Mike said. "It's worse in some areas."

And it was beginning to sting Mike's eyes. What was it doing to Roselle's?

It grew thicker and more toxic with each moment. Mike took in a breath, feeling like he had just swallowed kerosene.

What is that smell? He recognized it but couldn't give it a name. *Gas?* No. Then he remembered. He had smelled it hundreds of times while traveling on business. It was jet fuel.

Roselle panted harder. But not once did she stop, whine, or resist the forward movement.

"I wonder if there was a mid-air collision," a man suggested.

"Something hit the building," someone else said. "That would be too low for a plane to fly."

"It has happened before," an older man pointed out.

It had. Mike remembered reading about a B-25 bomber that hit the Empire State Building in 1945. The pilot was experienced and had earned many awards, but he got lost in thick fog and flew right into the 76th floor, killing 14 people, himself, and his two passengers.

It still didn't make sense. Once last night's storm passed, they had awoken to a clear day, not fog.

Mike, Roselle, David, and the others continued down as if in a group trance.

Ten stairs.

Turn.

Nine stairs.

♥ 🐕 ♥ 🐕 ♥

On the 70th floor, they had to leave the stairwell and move through the abandoned hallway to another set of stairs. The stairs began to fill up as more and more people decided to stop waiting for instructions and leave the building. Every once in a while Mike and Roselle had to move to the side as someone pushed past in an attempt to escape faster, but other than that, no one shoved, hurried, or ordered those ahead of them to move faster. No one had given them a reason to panic, so they exited in an orderly fashion just as they'd been instructed to do during fire drills. "If there is a need to evacuate the building, do not use the elevators unless specifically told to do so," they'd always been told. "Instead, go to the nearest stairwell and walk down to the bottom and exit as soon as you get there, or do whatever building personnel tell you to do at the bottom."

How long had they been on the stairs? Mike let go of the banister and felt under his sleeve for the numbers on his Braille watch. It was 8:55, only nine minutes since the explosion. It seemed like so much longer.

In an attempt to get his mind off the smell of fuel, Mike began to time their exit. The stairwell was beginning to heat up from the crowd. Mike's shirt stuck to his body. Roselle's breathing grew heavier.

At one second per step, it should take us about 22 minutes to reach the exit, not including slow-downs along the way.

Shouting from above stopped his calculations.

"Step aside! Burn victim! Let us through!"

Mike directed Roselle back as the smell of burnt clothing whooshed past him.

"David." He turned toward his friend. "What did you see?"

"A woman. She is burned badly."

Whatever happened, it was serious. There must be more people injured, but where are they?

The air was getting thicker and heavier with the stench of fuel.

Mike heard the quick frantic breathing of panic coming from a woman behind him.

"I can't breathe." She stopped in her tracks. "I don't think we're going to make it out of here. We're going to . . ."

The line came to a halt as people tried to reassure her.

"It's going to be okay."

"Take a deep breath. Relax. You can do it."

"We're going to make it."

Mike and David both reached toward the woman and gave her a hug. "Hey, it's going to be fine. We're going to get out."

Without prompting, Roselle nudged the woman's hand. Her panting was friendly and light. The women loosened her grip on Mike and reached down to pet Roselle's head. Her breathing slowed. She laughed.

"Thank you." She sniffed and took a deep breath. She gave Roselle another stroke. "And thank you."

"You ready?" Mike squeezed her arm.

"Yes. I'm fine now. Let's do this." She took her place in line and they all resumed walking.

Are we really going to make it out of here? Mike thought about Karen, home alone waiting for his call. How could he leave her behind? They needed each other. I'm her feet, God.

What about Ellery? Did he know what was happening?

Did Mr. Herboldsheimer, one of the best teachers and mentors he'd ever had, a teacher who had become such a close friend that he'd attended Mike and Karen's wedding? Would he ever see Mr. Herbo again?

He started using an old Boy Scout trick of touching the fire doors as they passed them. No heat. No fire, at least not on these lower floors.

They moved aside for another burn victim, then another.

Then someone else panicked. This time it was David.

"Mike," he stammered. "We're not going to make it out."

Mike tightened his grip on Roselle's harness, feeling her gaze up at him. She was still calm and he needed to keep it that way. If he freaked out, so would she.

"David." Mike moved closer and raised his voice,

fighting to keep himself together. "If Roselle and I can do it, so can you."

As he urged his friend to keep going, one fear nagged at him, a fear worse than the fire or the possibility of not making it out.

What if the lights go out? He had lived in the dark his whole life, but no one else on the stairs had. That would be the start of real panic. Total chaos.

He followed Roselle down a flight of 10 steps. She was panting so hard. This experience went beyond anything she had been trained for.

"Good girl, Roselle. You are doing such a great job." She must be so tired and thirsty.

He touched his watch. 9:05.

Wait! I've lived in the dark my whole life. That's the answer. If the lights go out, I'll be the one at an advantage, so I'll be the guide.

"People," he called out. "If the lights happen to go out, don't worry a bit. Roselle and I are offering a two-for-one special today and will get us all out of here."

"Well, that's a relief." A man chuckled.

For a moment, everyone was laughing and the mood lightened. Then they focused on the stairs again.

Ten stairs.

Turn.

Nine stairs.

It was getting hotter. Mike wiped his sweaty

forehead. "I hear walking is a great way to lose weight."

The laughter on the stairs started up again. Good, Mike thought. We need to keep our spirits up.

"I definitely need to lose a few pounds," the man behind Mike said through heavy breaths. Me, too, Mike admitted to himself.

"Well, I plan to have an extra dessert tonight," another man said.

"I plan to have dessert tonight," a lady added. "I earned it."

Mike got an idea. "On the first day that they let us back in the tower, we'll meet on the 78th floor at 8:45 and start our new weight loss program, walking the stairs."

David interrupted Mike to inform him that they had reached the 35th floor. Mike was about to tell the group how many they had to go when he heard noises coming from below.

"They're passing something up," David said. "Water bottles!"

Someone had broken into a vending machine and was passing cold bottles of water up to the parched group.

David placed a refreshingly cold bottle into Mike's palm. The cool water washed away the acidy taste of the fuel-drenched air. He felt Roselle's gaze, heard her thirsty pants. He swallowed one last swig then knelt beside her. Guide dogs didn't usually get water or food during the day, to prevent the need for potty breaks, but today the rules took a backseat to Roselle's needs.

He and David made a cup out of their hands to give Roselle water. She lapped at the water as fast as she could. When the bottle was empty, they all continued downstairs.

"Good, Roselle." Mike rubbed her face. Her nose was hot from exhaustion and dehydration. "You're such a good dog. Just keep going. We can do it, right?"

17

KISSING FIREFIGHTERS

Roselle

Roselle licked every drop of that wonderful water from her lips. *I need more, but Mike said to keep going, so that's what I'm going to do.*

Everyone on the stairwell was tense; she could feel it. The fear was as thick and strong as that horrible odor burning her nose and eyes. But Mike stayed calm as the others whispered and released their anxiety through heavy breaths. *If Mike was calm, there was no need to be afraid.*

"Everyone, move to the side," David shouted. "There are firefighters coming up the stairs."

"Finally!"

A line of emergency workers wearing heavy uniforms and fire gear rushed up the stairs. Roselle welcomed the chance to stop for a moment. As a puppy, walking down a few stairs had felt like the ultimate test. Todd had worked her on long flights of stairs during her training, but never so many at once. When will these stairs end?

"Hey, buddy." The first firefighter stopped in front of them and looked at Mike. "You okay?"

"I'm fine," Mike told him.

The firefighter reached down to pet Roselle. He must not know the rule, Roselle realized. For once, Mike didn't explain why it wasn't okay, so Roselle enjoyed the affection. He seemed like such a nice man, so brave to run up the stairs to where the danger was.

"I'm going to send someone down with you so you get out okay," the firefighter told Mike.

"No, I'm really okay. I have my dog."

Roselle gave the man a curious stare. Anyone who knew Mike knew he didn't need extra help just because he couldn't see. Besides, helping Mike was her job. The firefighter had other people to save— people who were hurt or trapped, or burned like those people who'd been carried down the stairs. Mike wouldn't want to take him away from those who needed his help more.

"Nice dog, by the way."

Roselle nosed the man's hand as a way of saying thank you, and he continued petting her.

The firefighter kept insisting on getting Mike some help, and Mike continued to refuse it.

"Hey, you can't get lost going downstairs," Mike joked. "Besides, my friend David is with me and he can see just fine."

"We're okay," David assured the firefighter.

The man finally shrugged and gave up.

"Can we help you guys with anything?" Mike asked.

"No, but thanks. We're good." The firefighter gave Roselle one last pat. She kissed his hand with her nose. Then he was gone, along with the rest of his crew.

What was happening up there? Not even the firefighters seemed to know.

"Forward," Mike told Roselle as more firefighters began streaming up the stairs.

Roselle forced her weary legs forward, her eyes on the steps ahead, feeling the rising heat penetrate her fur, hearing the thump of the firefighter's boots grow quieter and quieter, sensing the vibration of hundreds of feet through her tender paws, along with the intensifying fear. *Just keep moving forward. If Mike says we can do this, we can.*

Down.

Turn.

Down.

She repeated this routine over and over again,

trying hard not to let the conversations between Mike and David and the rest of the people distract her. She couldn't think about being thirsty or tired. All that matters is getting Mike down the stairs and out of the tower. Then we can rest.

There were so many more people on the stairs than when they first started, and more people meant moving more slowly, which seemed to make everyone nervous. More firefighters raced up, so they moved to the side again. Everyone applauded for them. David slapped a firefighter on the back and thanked him.

Again, they offered Mike extra help and he politely said, "No thanks."

"Mike," David said, "I am going to walk down and stay a floor ahead of you. I can be an advanced lookout." Then David was gone.

Suddenly Mike heard David call up, "I'm on the 28th floor. Everything is okay here."

He continued to count down the floors staying one floor below Mike. The sound of David's voice seemed to reassure everyone, giving them something to focus on besides being afraid.

"Forward," Mike said again. And Roselle moved forward, panting to release the heat in her body.

"10th floor," David called.

They met yet another group on the stairwell and moved even more slowly. The men and women grew even more anxious, all except Mike who remained calm. Every once in a while, Roselle sensed what felt like fear coming from her handler, but then he would settle down again.

"Good girl," he kept saying. "You're doing great."

So she kept going. Until finally, she heard something. It sounded like rain, heavy rain, but inside instead of outside.

"Floor one," David shouted. "We made it."

"Yes!" Someone shouted.

"Thank you, God!"

"The sprinklers are on," David warned, "so get ready for a shower."

Roselle picked up her pace as Mike directed her toward the door leading out of the stairwell into the lower lobby. The whole group sucked in the cool air at once. No more smell of jet fuel; no more crowded stairs; no more walking down, down. We are almost out.

Water gushed over the tile floor. Roselle's paws splashed in the water as they exited the stairwell. Her tongue could almost feel it. She had known the rule about not eating or drinking from the ground since her puppy years, but she was so thirsty that her natural instinct pushed aside her training, and she lunged, dipping her nose into the stream. It smelled funny and looked cloudy, but she didn't care. It was water.

Before she could take even one sip, Mike pulled her back. "Roselle, no."

He allowed me to drink on the stairs. Why not now?

"Forward," Mike shouted, and everyone started to run through the waterfall, shrieks of shock from the cold water mixed with sighs of relief. Water bathed Roselle's face. She licked the drops that rolled down her muzzle.

Finally, they were standing in the middle of the lobby. They'd made it. Emergency workers ran in and up the same stairs Roselle and Mike had just come down. Injured men and women hobbled toward the door or were carried by friends or firefighters. Ceiling tiles, soaked file folders, coffee cups, and other fallen items floated past Roselle's paws. A lady dropped her jacket while rushing to the revolving door and didn't stop to pick it up. Everyone looked lost and confused.

Mike reached down and rubbed Roselle's aching body, praising her. She felt Mike tense up as if he knew what was coming next. He knew dogs well, right down to what happened right after they got wet.

Roselle shook her drenched head and let the shakes ripple down her body and out the tip of her tail. *That felt good!*

Mike laughed and shook his soaked arms. "Yeah,

there you go, Roselle. Shake it off." He dried his face with his jacket.

"We need to go." David tugged Mike's arm. "Whatever is going on, this place is like a war zone."

"Come on, Roselle." Mike picked up the harness again. "Let's get outside and call Karen. We need to get home."

18

GLASS WATERFALLS AND SMOKE CLOUDS

Mike

"FBI," a man said as soon as Mike reached the doorway with Roselle and David. "I'll show you where to go."

He directed them through the revolving doors and into the underground shopping area, to avoid putting people in danger from falling debris. More sprinklers and ankle-deep water awaited them there, along with more commotion. From the sounds and smells and chaos around him, all Mike knew was they needed to get outside as quickly as possible.

They followed the crowd through the entire length of the underground center to the escalator, going up to the outdoor plaza on the other side of the

World Trade Center.

Mike stopped to breathe. Outdoor air at last. But it didn't smell fresh. Not at all.

"Oh, wow." David rested his hand on Mike's arm. "There's a fire in Tower Two, up high."

How was that possible? Something had clearly hit Tower One. Had the fire in Tower Two been so powerful that they felt it in Tower One? Had it jumped and spread?

Waves of people brushed past Mike and David. Mike pulled Roselle back a little.

"You guys okay?" A paramedic approached.

"We're fine," David said. "No injuries. Let's get out of the way, Mike."

"W-ABC News," a woman ran alongside Mike. "Can you tell me what you experienced in there?"

Feeling an urgent need to get away from the fire, Mike waved her off and kept moving.

They stopped for a moment on the corner of Broadway and Ann. David took out his phone, held it up, and snapped a picture of the fire. Mike took his phone out and dialed home. Karen needed to know he was out and safe.

"All circuits are currently busy." Mike remembered the mob on the stairs. How many of them were trying to call home at this exact moment, along with thousands from Tower Two? Of course the circuits were busy.

David had just snapped another picture and Mike was putting his phone back in his pocket when a policeman ran toward them.

"Get out of here. Now! It's coming down!"

What is coming down? Then he heard it.

A deep rumble from Tower Two crescendoed to a deafening roar, like the combined sound of a giant freight train headed straight toward them and a waterfall of shattering glass. Mike suddenly felt like he was standing on a giant concrete trampoline as vibrations rippled up his legs, paralyzing him with horror. He opened his mouth but no scream came out.

David shouted and took off running. Mike turned around, clutched Roselle's harness, picked her up off her feet, and swung her around as they joined the screaming, terrified crowd, running as fast as they could, away from the falling tower. Unlike on the stairs, no one stopped to offer help. It was every man and woman for themselves—except for Mike and Roselle; they had each other.

Metal and glass fell around them, along with pebbles of concrete and tiny objects that pelted Mike's face and head.

He thought of Karen. *God, what if I die? I didn't get to say goodbye to her.*

He ran from the noise, but his mind screamed to God. *How could this happen? Why would you get us out of the building only to have it fall on us?*

God immediately answered, speaking directly to Mike's frightened heart.

Don't worry about what you cannot control. Focus on running with Roselle, and the rest will take care of itself.

Mike had never heard God speak so clearly or felt Him so close. He actually heard a voice in his head and felt calmed by that voice. With pieces of Tower Two raining around him, Mike felt God's peace and protection surrounding him while he and Roselle did the only thing they could—keep running.

They reached Fulton Street, and somehow Mike and Roselle found David again. They all stopped, fighting to catch their breath.

"You okay, Roselle?" Mike ran his hands over her dusty coat, feeling the rapid racing of her heart. She licked her lips between pants and blew out gusts of filthy air through her nose. "You're amazing today, girl."

But it wasn't over. The falling glass and metal was immediately followed by a monstrous cloud that enveloped the three in concrete dust, gas, and smoke. Mike had no choice but to take in a deep breath and start running again. Roselle took the lead without hesitation, doing her job like it was any other day.

We're in this together, Mike reminded himself as he clutched Roselle's harness and ducked his head against the toxic cloud. If they lived through this day or died, they would not let go of each other.

Karen was praying for him; he knew it. He and David walked for a while then ran again, desperate to get away from the cloud. Yet even in the dust, he felt God's presence.

"Roselle, right," he called whenever he sensed an open doorway. He could tell by the pull of Roselle's harness that she was on the lookout too. Finally Mike heard an opening. "Right."

Roselle turned right, but then she stopped. It was first time she had stopped without Mike's permission all day. Mike knew guide dogs well enough to understand that she wouldn't do such a thing without a reason. It was the intelligent disobedience they taught about at Guide Dogs for the Blind.

Mike reached out and felt a handrail. He extended his right foot and felt the edge of a step. This wasn't a doorway; it was a flight of stairs.

Roselle sneezed again and again.

Mike directed Roselle forward. What was one more flight?

David followed them down. He rubbed his eyes. "We're at the Fulton Street Subway Station," he said once he could see clearly enough to read the sign.

At the bottom of the stairs, they found a small space that turned out to be an arcade. They heard a woman crying.

"I can't see," she wailed. "My eyes are so full of dirt. I can't see! I don't want to fall into the subway track."

Mike nudged Roselle's harness. This was another moment when he was the one at an advantage. He reached out and touched the woman's arms. Her cries quieted. He gently tucked her arm into his.

"My name is Mike. I'm blind and I have my guide dog, Roselle, with me. We'll make sure you don't fall."

Roselle stood still, watching the woman.

"Thank you." The woman clutched Mike's arm as they made their way through the station, the blind leading the blind.

A man who worked for the subway ran over and introduced himself as Lou. "Follow me." Others followed, all people who had run from the falling tower.

Lou took the group to the employee locker room, where there was a fan going and a water fountain. They took turns washing their faces and drinking from the fountain. Water never tasted so wonderful. Roselle flopped to the ground for a rest.

Mike's mind spun. *How many people have died or been injured? What if David and I had stayed in the office longer to save our files? We would still be on the stairwell right now.*

♥ 🐕 ♥ 🐕 ♥

They had barely recovered when a police officer entered the locker room. "I'm sorry to say this, but they ordered me to evacuate the station," he told the group. "The air is clearing."

They headed out again. Back out on the street, the dust had settled. People were quiet.

They continued down Fulton Street, away from the fallen tower, walking as if stuck in a bad dream. According to David, Tower One was on fire but still standing. It would probably be a while before they got to return to their office.

Mike brushed off his clothes and raked his fingers through his hair to remove the dirt.

"You have blood on your face," David told him.

Mike touched his face, remembering the glass and the rocks and the dust cloud.

They had been walking for about 10 minutes when it happened again. Mike heard a second roar, another freight train and waterfall of glass. Again, the ground vibrated. Roselle pressed against Mike's leg. They were far enough away to avoid the danger this time. But inside, Mike's heart tore in half. Tower One— their tower—was crumbling to the ground.

None of them had the energy to run anymore. A deep sadness hung over the small group. The World Trade Center had collapsed, and how many people had died along with it? Mike remembered the FBI man who directed them out and all those firefighters that passed them on the stairs. Did any of them get out in time? What about that firefighter who stopped to pet Roselle? I'm so glad I didn't make him stop, or give a lecture about the rules. Mike leaned against the building behind him. Petting Roselle and feeling her kiss his hand was the last moment of affection that man ever experienced.

Mike stroked Roselle's head. He had asked for a dog that could focus when it was time to work and play once the harness came off. He'd never expected to get one who also knew when to kiss a firefighter.

The roar stopped. Another dust cloud engulfed the streets, but this time it was too far away to touch them.

Another loss hit Mike, one that seemed minor compared to human lives, but one that still hurt deeply. The Braillewriter that Mom and Dad bought him so many years ago—the one that went with him to school from fourth grade on up through college— the tool that felt like such a part of him that he'd kept it on display in his office—was somewhere in the burning rubble. How can I even think about something like that? People died, and I'm worried about my Braillewriter? But he and Roselle were safe, and so was his friend David. The guests from the conference room had left minutes before he and David did, so they were alive too.

"There is no more World Trade Center," David

said. His voice shook.

Mike knew he should be happy to be alive, and he was grateful. But how could he be happy when so many others didn't make it out? All he could feel was numbness.

Karen. His heart racing, he pulled out his phone and tried one more time. It rang once, twice, three times. *She needs to know I'm alive.*

"Hello." Her voice sounded so hollow and small, so sad.

"Karen?" His throat felt almost too tight to speak. "It's me, Mike."

He could hear her crying.

"I'm okay." Mike had never been much of a crier, even as a kid, but hearing Karen's voice after all that had happened made it impossible to fight the tears and sobs. "Roselle and I made it out."

As much as he loved Roselle, Karen was the one who made him feel completely whole. They both knew what it felt like to live with limitation and need help when they'd rather do everything on their own. Mike knew he drove Karen crazy sometimes, but none of that mattered on the day when they almost lost each other.

Through Karen, they learned what happened. A terrorist group had taken over four airplanes, maybe even more. The first had hit Tower One. Ten minutes later, a second had hit Tower Two. They had flown a third plane into the Pentagon.

"Another plane is still missing," Karen said.

All airplanes were grounded. The president was in hiding for his own safety. The whole city was in chaos and people across the world were glued to their televisions.

What was happening? Would the world ever be the same?

Roselle nudged his leg. They needed to get out of this area.

"I love you, Karen." Mike wiped his eyes. "I'll be home as soon as I can."

The question was, how would they get there?

19

A BRUSH, A BONE, AND HOME

Roselle

Roselle stared in the direction of the settling cloud and the smoky, burning empty space that had once been two giant towers. The air smelled like so many bad things that she couldn't sort them out. She sneezed again. She shook to release the dirt from her ears, but they still felt clogged. No matter how many times she shook, her coat held a layer of ash. She licked her lips, but they tasted bitter and dirty.

She dropped to the down position. Mike and David were so quiet and so sad. Mike was hardly ever quiet, and she'd never seen him cry before today. She rested her head in her paws, sensing that it was not yet time to close her eyes. Any minute now, Mike would say, "Roselle, up" then "Forward" and they would be on their way again. Hopefully this time, they wouldn't have to run.

"Let's see if we can get some news." Mike pulled a small portable radio out of his brief case. The voice coming out of the speaker told everyone to remain calm. He said something about terrorists crashing planes into buildings. So that was what happened. That was why they had to run from the water and the glass and the smoke. That was why Mike's office disappeared.

Why would anyone want to do such a horrible thing?

Other voices came on the radio, asking the man questions. As David and Mike talked, Roselle learned that those people were reporters, and the man answering the questions was the mayor of New York.

Roselle's eyes grew heavier until she couldn't keep them open any more. The voices on Mike's radio lulled her to sleep.

Then she felt a tug on her harness. It was time to go.

"I know a woman who lives in Manhattan," David told Mike. "Her name is Nina. I'll see if she is home."

Nina told David that she could meet them at her apartment in a couple of hours, so they walked some more while they waited. At noon, they found a small

Vietnamese restaurant. Roselle rested at Mike's feet.

"I can't eat anything." David pushed his menu aside.

Mike ordered soup for both himself and David. Roselle felt him relax as he slowly ate. She'd heard that soup did that to people. She could tell he was still a bit wound up though. She let her head fall against Mike's leg. Maybe that will help him calm down more.

A loud roar coming from the sky woke Roselle so abruptly that she almost hit her head on Mike chair. Mike's body stiffened.

"Planes." Mike dropped his spoon.

David and others ran to the door and looked outside. David craned his neck. "It's the Air Force. Our planes are patrolling the skies."

Everyone in the restaurant cheered.

"At least now we feel a little safer." Mike sipped his cup of tea.

When it came time to go to Nina's, they walked again, until some people in a van offered them a ride. They didn't speak English very well, but they seemed to know what happened and wanted to help.

Nina wasn't at her apartment when they arrived, so they sat in the hall and Roselle prepared for another snooze.

"I wish I could join you," Mike said, stroking her ears.

It wasn't long before Mike woke Roselle. She opened one eye at a time and saw a lady hurrying down the hallway, her arms loaded down with groceries.

"I'm so sorry." She stopped to catch her breath. "But I wanted to get you guys some food. You should've seen the grocery store. It was an absolute zoo. Everyone was in a panic, trying to stock up on as much as possible."

David took the bags out of her arms so she could unlock the door.

Roselle sat up. Oh, a new friend. Nina looked nice. She wagged her tail and followed Nina into the apartment.

It felt so good to finally be inside a safe, clean room. When Mike unclipped Roselle's harness, she felt free. She stretched her front legs then her hind legs. Then she followed Nina into the living room.

"Nina, meet Roselle," Mike said. "The bravest dog in the world."

♥ 🐕 ♥ 🐕 ♥

A couple hours later, Mike phoned Karen again then called for Roselle. It was time to go home, or at least try. By now, they had learned that the missing plane had crash-landed in a Pennsylvania field.

They rode a bus to Penn Station to catch the subway. David and Mike stopped to say goodbye.

They had to part quickly, but Roselle heard tears in their voices. They had been through so much together. Roselle watched David walk away, his shirt coated with ash.

The station was packed with people, all talking about where they were when the towers fell.

When they reached the station in New Jersey, they transferred to a second train. They got off, and Karen's van pulled up at the curb. Karen wasn't driving but sitting in her wheelchair in the center of the van. A friend had come to be with Karen earlier in the day and offered to drive her to meet Mike. Karen slid the door open. Mike and Roselle piled in.

Karen and Mike reached their arms out to each other, hugging so tightly that Roselle wondered if they would ever let go. They gave each other a kiss then hugged again. Tears poured down Karen's cheeks.

Roselle found a spot on the floor as the van pulled away from the curb.

Finally, they pulled up to the house. Before Karen had a chance to wheel herself through the doorway, Linnie ran to greet them all. Roselle prepared for the attack from her best dog friend.

Linnie! She panted with joy.

But instead of jumping on her, Linnie sniffed Roselle all over. Next she sniffed Mike.

"Let's get you cleaned up." Mike removed Roselle's

harness. Something about being home recharged Roselle's batteries. She no longer felt tired. In fact, she couldn't wait to run. She spotted a familiar rope sticking out from under the coffee table. My Booda Bone! She made a run for it.

"Okay, you win." Mike finally let go. "You've earned some playtime. Grooming can wait. I need a shower anyway."

Roselle snatched the bone, shaking it with all her strength, sending more dust into the air. Linnie ran over and grabbed the other end of the rope toy. Back and forth they tugged. News played in the background, and Roselle and Linnie went right on tugging. And as they tugged, the sounds and images from the day began to fade from Roselle's mind.

20

FORWARD

Mike, September 12, 2001

Mike could barely move when he woke up the next morning. Every muscle in his body ached; even his hands hurt. His stiff legs screamed for mercy as he slowly forced them over the side of the bed. He moaned, gritting his teeth.

He pulled on his robe, stuffed his feet into his slippers, and shuffled over to untie Linnie and Roselle, who immediately started a game of chase. Where did she get her energy after such a traumatic day? While the dogs tore down the steps to the basement, Mike took Karen's elevator downstairs. He opened the back door to take out the dogs before they woke Karen. His calf muscles burned with every step as he walked each dog, wishing his backyard had a fence so he could stand still while they did their morning business. He then went up to the kitchen where he boiled water for tea and popped an English muffin in the toaster. He was spreading butter on his muffin when the truth hit him: he no longer had an office to go back to today. He would never go to room 7827 again, never walk through the sky lobby, and never order those heavenly ham and cheese croissants. There were people he would never say good morning to again or chat with in the elevator. *So many people.*

The horrible sounds from the day before replayed in Mike's mind. Once again, he and Roselle were running for their lives from flying glass and debris. He heard the screams of the hundreds of men and women desperate to get as far away from the falling tower as possible. He rubbed his face, trying to shake off the memories. His grip on the butter knife tightened.

He took a deep breath and went back to spreading butter. For now, he just wanted to do something normal like enjoy his breakfast. He would have to face reality eventually, but he wasn't ready yet.

Mike, Karen, and their friend, Tom Painter, spent the day resting, listening to the news, and answering phone call after phone call while Roselle and Linnie played like nothing unusual had happened.

Ellery called around 10 in the morning. The night before, Mike had received a call from his former pastor, who encouraged him to pray and relax in order to absorb what had happened and begin the process of moving on. But there was little time for that today. Ellery's call was one of many that Wednesday morning, and with every call Mike shared his story of escaping with Roselle.

After talking on the phone for hours, he thought of one more person who needed to know he'd made it out of the World Trade Center safely.

Before he got a chance to make that call, the phone rang. "Mike, it's Mr. Herbo." His former teacher's voice quivered with emotions. "It's so good to hear your voice."

Mike started to tell Mr. Herbo the whole story, but the calls were coming in so often that they had to put off their talk until later. For now, it was just good to hear from his friend.

After hanging up, Mike turned his attention back to Roselle. Other than still being a bit dirty and smelly, Roselle had bounced back to her old pixie-like self. Mike listened to her romps, skids, and happy barks. If she seemed upset about anything it was that Linnie had hidden the Booda Bone and she couldn't find it. Will reality hit her later? *How will she act when we return to a normal everyday routine? Will every boom and playful scream rattle her nerves? Will she still be able to do her job?*

Karen suggested that Mike call Guide Dogs for the

Blind to let them know he was okay and ask about his concerns. He dialed the number and once again told his story.

"How can I help her recover from this?" he asked just as Roselle found the hidden Booda Bone. She began thumping it on the hardwood floor and Linnie attempted to grab it, prompting another chase. Obviously, she wasn't in any physical pain. "She must be traumatized."

"You'd be surprised," a veterinarian known as Doc Dietrich said. "One nice thing about dogs is that they live in the moment. Labrador retrievers are extremely adaptable and able to bounce back from frightening events. This might sound strange after all you've been through, but what happened yesterday is over for Roselle."

He'd heard that dogs were resilient, but he'd also heard stories about guide dogs that could no longer lead well after a traumatic experience. But Doc explained that since she was not hurt and hadn't been attacked personally, she would most likely move on. All he could do was trust this expert's words and Roselle's behavior, and pray for the best.

Next on the to-do list was to call his doctor and Roselle's vet. He was already hearing reports of toxic fumes and particles in the dust clouds that followed each falling tower. Mike's doctor prescribed an antibiotic to fight any infections that might be lurking in his lungs. But the vet didn't suggest any special treatment for Roselle.

"All she needs right now is rest and routine."

Mike finally tackled Roselle for a much-needed brushing. If only his experience could also be erased by rest and routine. Why couldn't humans move on as quickly as dogs did? Or maybe there were some things we weren't supposed to forget.

Karen looked out the window. "I can see the smoke from the World Trade Center, and we're more than thirty miles away."

News covered the search for survivors. All American flights were grounded, filling the air over the United States with an eerie silence. New Yorkers posted pictures of loved ones that they hoped were still alive in the rubble or a local hospital. Some were; others weren't.

Mike began to see some good come out of his experience when he received an unexpected phone call from Joanne Ritter at Guide Dogs for the Blind. They had already sent out a mass e-mail to all of their employees, as well as the Sterns, sharing Mike and Roselle's story.

"I'd like to get your story out to the media," Joanne said. "Would you be willing to be interviewed?"

"Sure," Mike said without really thinking. He wouldn't mind sharing his experience, but with thousands of escape stories, who would want to listen to his?

♥ 🐕 ♥ 🐕 ♥

On Friday, only three days after descending 78 flights of stairs with Roselle and hearing his former workplace crumble in an avalanche of glass and metal, Mike, Roselle, Karen, and Tom Painter sat in the green room at CNN Studios in New York City. As willing as he was to share his experience, Mike felt more overwhelmed than he ever had in his life. The reality of going from an ordinary day to a nightmare was sinking in, along with the knowledge that he would soon be telling his story to the world while being interviewed by one of the most recognizable men on television. Why did I say yes to this?

But once the interview began, Mike saw the benefits of sharing what he went through, with Roselle sitting at his side. The interviewer, a man named Larry King, was warm and engaging, focusing the interview on Mike's blindness and his relationship with Roselle. As Mike spoke, he realized that he was offering a hurting, unsettled world a message of hope that he also needed. The longer he spoke, the more he felt his mood shifting from overwhelmed to thankful for the opportunity.

As Mike relived the morning of September 11 in his mind again and again, he realized how differently things could have played out for him and Roselle and

David. If he and David had stayed behind longer or tried to help others evacuate, they would've gone down with the tower. Remembering all the falling debris, he knew it was a miracle that he, David, and his precious dog got away without being struck by anything except tiny pebbles and shards of glass that didn't even require stitches.

Among the thousands who did not survive were a few men and women with disabilities, who were simply following instructions they'd been given during emergency drills to go to a specific place and wait for rescue. Mike's determination to always have a plan for emergencies that did not include waiting around for help had saved his life.

The more the truth sank in, the more Mike battled anger toward the 19 men who hijacked and purposely crashed those airplanes full of innocent passengers and crewmembers, knowing they would kill thousands in the process. *How could they have such a lack of regard for life? Were they even human?*

God, I'll never understand it.

It would take a long time to work through his grief, and he knew it. But one of the many lessons his parents had taught him was the importance of moving forward when tragedy hit. It was one thing to grieve and another to wallow and stay stuck in the fear and pain. He had never allowed anything to hold him back, and he wouldn't allow what evil men did hold him back from living a full life now.

While many survivors struggled with feelings of guilt that they survived while others died, Mike chose to not let himself feel guilty. Other than the fact that he followed his instincts, took cues from Roselle, and knew in his heart that God was with him even before he heard His voice of assurance, there was no explanation for why he and Roselle survived while others did not. No matter how special and focused Roselle had always been, her response remained unexplainable. All he knew was God allowed him to survive for a reason, and he would not let that purpose go to waste. God had used him that day to calm that frightened lady on the stairwell, shake some sense into David when he thought they would never get out alive, settle fears over the possibility of the lights going out, and help a women who had been blinded by the dust. He had also used Roselle, who knew when to run for their lives and when to stop long enough to give a firefighter one last kiss.

He quickly began to receive reminders that his television interview had made a difference too. Other requests for interviews came, including newspapers, radio programs, and television shows, all wanting to hear about the blind man who made it down 78 flights of stairs with a guide dog named Roselle. At first he hesitated. Why was his escape story such a big deal compared to the countless others who had walked the same stairs? But he knew the answer—his story was considered extraordinary because he was blind and accompanied by a guide dog. Accepting these interviews would allow him to talk about the skills he'd learned while growing up without sight, all of which helped him on that life-changing Tuesday morning.

When he appeared on television, Roselle took to the spotlight and was treated like a hero. As Mike retold his experience, he felt healing that so often comes with talking through a frightening event and realizing that you are okay. Not only that, but he had a positive story to tell about a horrible day—something that Americans needed. These interviews also allowed him to introduce the world to an ordinary, hard-working man who happened to be blind. They opened the door for him to talk about living with blindness, guide dogs, and the partnership that allowed him and Roselle to escaped Tower One.

Mike went back to work, but quickly discovered that the September 11th attack had changed him. His work at Quantum and making money no longer seemed important. When Guide Dogs for the Blind offered him a job that would allow him to use his story of escaping the World Trade Center to educate others about the importance of guide dogs and the guide dog/handler relationship, he accepted it. This would mean moving back to California and working on the campus where he had received his first guide dog and met Roselle.

His willingness to talk about his experience also led to exciting things for Roselle.

In the early part of 2002, Mike heard from a British organization called the PDSA (Pet Dispensary for Sick Animals). The PDSA was formed as a charity by Maria Dickin in 1919 to care for sick and injured animals in England. The PDSA also created a way to recognize animals that performed heroic efforts during wartime, and they wanted to honor Roselle.

She would receive the Dickin Award during a ceremony in New York on March 5, 2002. Another guide dog from Tower One, Salty, would also receive an award, along with a German shepherd named Apollo, who would represent all the search and rescue dogs who worked so hard on 9/11.

The ceremony took place near Ground Zero, the new name for the site where the World Trade Center once stood. Mike and Karen accompanied Roselle as she received her medal. After the ceremony, everyone was invited to a celebration at the British Consulate. Mike and Karen were overwhelmed with the hugeness of the event and pride in their incredible dog; Roselle just wagged her tail and took it all in stride. Mike sensed that she knew she had done a good job and that she was loved, but the day was much more special to the humans in her life, who understood how different this day could have been.

21

RETIRED HERO

Roselle, 2004-2007

Roselle lay in her new favorite spot beside Mike and Karen's sliding glass door overlooking their backyard. The warm sun poured in, relaxing her tired body. From the moment she and Mike appeared on television for the first time, life had completely changed. Now, when people heard the name Roselle they thought of a day known as 9/11, a day she no longer remembered, but Mike would clearly never forget.

They had appeared on many TV and radio shows, including some that were broadcast in other countries. They posed for newspaper and magazine articles, and even a book about September 11, 2001 published by Time magazine. Mike and Karen had a shelf full of awards presented to Roselle by organizations like the PDSA, American Kennel Club, the British Guide Dogs Association, and The Little Rock Foundation. Shortly after receiving the Dickin Award, she had won the AKA Canine Excellence Award.

People seemed to think she was some kind of hero, but Roselle didn't feel like one. She had just been doing her job when she and Mike walked down those stairs. She hadn't done all the work; they'd done it together like always. Mike reminded people of that often—that she hadn't saved him that day, they worked as a team. Others called her special because she didn't panic. When she heard Mike tell their story and people in the audience gasped and looked shocked, she understood that he was talking about something scary, but she couldn't remember ever being with Mike in a moment when she felt like panicking, expect maybe when Cali or Sherlock hissed at her from under the bed. Even then she knew it was just a game.

Hero or not, the attention was a lot of fun. Roselle loved meeting so many new people and getting her picture taken. Photographers referred to her as photogenic, and many of the people she met were very important. She didn't really care if they were famous or not as long as they were nice. She especially loved going to the Guide Dogs for the Blind campus where Mike worked. She got to see old friends like Todd and Dave. Living in California meant they got to see Ted and Kay, who always had a new guide dog puppy-in-training with them when they visited.

But today, as Roselle rested in her favorite sunny place, she felt tired. As exciting as it was to fly on airplanes and be on television and listen to Mike telling stories of a frightening day when they both could've died, all the travel was beginning to wear her out. Why didn't she have the energy for all the fun anymore?

Maybe she just felt draggy because she no longer had anyone to play tug with. Soon after moving from New York to California, Linnie had died. Roselle missed her friend terribly, and the house was so quiet without her. She still had Cali and Sherlock, but they didn't care about tug toys. All they did was sit and lick their paws. Cali was her buddy, but Sherlock usually looked at her like she was an intruder.

A dog named Panama came to live with them for a while, but she was old and had arthritis, so she didn't like to play very much. Maybe she was getting old too.

One morning as Roselle dozed for the third time since being released from her tether, Mike sat on the couch waving her Booda Bone.

"Roselle, come." Mike held out the toy. Her back ached as she stood. She tried to run but could only manage a walk. She grabbed the end of the rope and tugged, but after a few minutes, she let Mike win.

"Hey, girl, what's going on?" Mike rubbed her ears.

Karen wheeled over. "She just isn't her old perky self lately."

"I think it's time to take her to the vet. She moves a lot slower when she's guiding too."

So, in March of 2004, Mike and Roselle traveled to the vet at Guide Dogs for the Blind.

"It's nice to work in a place where we have our own personal vet," Mike pointed out on the way to their appointment.

After a number of pokes and prods, Doc sat across from Mike and Roselle, and explained that there was something wrong with her blood.

"Her platelet levels are dropping."

Roselle listened as Doc explained that she had something called immune-mediated thrombocytopenia. Roselle's body was attacking and destroying parts of her blood.

"I have no idea what is causing it." Doc stared down at Roselle. She gave him a pitiful look in return. She didn't care what was causing it; she just wanted to feel better so she could play tug and have the energy to do a good job for Mike.

When they got home, Mike told Karen what he thought caused Roselle's illness. "It was all that dust and the particles Roselle inhaled when the towers collapsed."

Doc found a set of medications that helped Roselle get her old bounce back. Once again, she had the energy and focus she needed to guide and travel with Mike, and life felt normal again.

Another yellow Lab from Guide Dogs for the Blind, named Fantasia, came to live with them in Panama's place. Fantasia's litters were used as puppies-in-training.

But in 2007, Roselle started to slow down again.

"Her blood levels are dropping," the vet said as he stroked Roselle's head. "I think it might be time to retire her. Guiding is extremely stressful work for a dog. These wonderful dogs always want to do a good job, and all that focus takes a lot of energy."

"Roselle takes her job very seriously." Mike patted Roselle's back.

Roselle could tell from the look on Mike's face that he didn't like the idea of retiring her, and she didn't like the sound of the word. It sounded so final. But she also knew she was tired.

On March 7, 2007, Roselle retired in a ceremony at Guide Dogs for the Blind. The entire staff attended. Even TV and newspaper reporters covered the event. An imprint of her paw was stamped into the cement in front of the administration building.

In August, Roselle received what Mike and Karen

called her highest honor. In a special meeting for Guide Dogs for the Blind's board of directors, the name Roselle was retired forever. Never again would Guide Dogs for the Blind give the name Roselle to one of their dogs. Roselle sat beside Mike during the ceremony and listened to a man explain that this had never been done before. Mike and Karen looked so happy and proud, but Roselle took it in like she did everything else, smiling and wagging her tail as if the ceremony was nothing more than another fun adventure.

♥

EXTRAS

WHERE ARE THEY NOW?

Twelve years after surviving the September 11, 2001 attack, Michael Hingson continues to travel around the world with his guide do Africa (who happens to be one of Fantasia's puppies), sharing his story of escaping Tower One of the World Trade Center with Roselle. He uses his experience as a tool for teaching the importance of teamwork and trust, the tight bond between guide dogs and blind people, and what we can learn from 9/11. His talks allow him the opportunity to share about what it's really like to be blind, clear up common misunderstandings, about disabilities, and encourage people to examine their prejudices, particularly when it comes to those living with physical challenges. Mike is now known as one of the top ten educational and motivational speakers in the world. So much for the doctor's prediction that he would never be able to do anything for himself!

In August 2011, Mike wrote a book with Susy Flory about his escape from The World Trade Center. *Thunder Dog* quickly made its way to the New York Times Bestseller List and has been translated into dozens of different languages, including German,

Japanese, Chinese, Finnish, and Portuguese.

Also in 2011, Mike started Roselle's Dream Foundation, dedicated to educating people about blindness and collecting funds so blind children can get the tools they need to make life and learning easier. He hopes to also make this help available to blind adults.

Roselle continued to win awards and attention long after her retirement 2007. She even got her own Facebook page that continues to draw likes. Sadly, her health continued to deteriorate. On June 26, 2011, Roselle passed away at age 14. After her death, Mike wrote a tribute to the friend and partner who would always be remembered for her heroism on one of America's darkest days. "How can I ever do justice to her life, work, and memory? Roselle has been one of the greatest blessings and gifts I have ever had the joy to let into my life. God surely broke the mold when she came into the world."

In October 2011, almost four months after her death, Roselle received an incredible honor when she won the American Humane Association's Hero Dog Award for her courage on September 11. Mike and his guide dog Africa accepted the award in her honor.

As Mike says, "There will never be another Roselle."

Sign up for Mike's newsletter at www.michaelhingson.com to keep up to date with his efforts. If you want to contact Mike, you can write to him at mike@michaelhingson.com.

WHAT A BLIND PERSON WANTS YOU TO KNOW

1. Please introduce yourself when you see me, even if we have met before. Eventually, I will recognize your voice, but I have a lot of voices to keep straight.

2. I am just like you; I just can't see as well. Talk to me and treat me as you would anyone else. If you need to know what I want (for example, do I want vanilla ice cream or chocolate), ask me, not my parent, friend, or spouse. Believe me, I know what I like. Oh, and there's no need to speak in a loud voice. I can hear just fine.

3. Feel free to use words like "see" and to talk about colors and other visual things. I enjoy knowing what the world around me looks like. It's okay to tell me I look nice. Who doesn't love a compliment?

4. I don't mind answering questions about blindness (in fact, feel free to ask anything you want), but I enjoy talking about ordinary everyday topics even more. Like any other person, I go to movies, have hobbies, and might even work or serve in my community. We probably have a lot in common.

5. I like to do as much as possible on my own. It

is fine to ask, "Can I help you with that?" but take my word for it if I say, "I can do it." If I need help, I promise to speak up.

6. It might be tempting to guide me along by grabbing my arm. That actually doesn't help me at all. Instead, offer your arm for me to hold.

7. If I have a guide dog, please don't pet him or her when the harness is on. A guide dog in harness is working. If I have a white cane, please don't play with it. This is what helps me move around independently.

8. Please let me know who is in the room, including pets. I also appreciate knowing about obstacles like steps without handrails, open car doors, and toys scattered on the floor.

9. Please include me in your conversations, games, and activities. I might play the game or do the activity a bit differently, but I still like to participate, and I love to discuss things.

10. There is no need to feel sorry for me or consider my accomplishments more remarkable than a sighted person's. Everyone has challenges; mine happens to be blindness.

11.

BLIND PEOPLE HAVE
THE COOLEST TOYS!

In addition to the Braillewriter, Talking Books, and screen readers that Mike used, check out other amazing tools that help blind people do the same things that you enjoy.

Reading and Writing - Back in the 1800s, the slate and stylus, which the blind use to punch Braille dots through a flat strip fitted over a piece of paper, was considered cutting edge. The typewriter-like Braillewriter came on the scene next. While these tools are still used today, blind students and adults can also use devices like Braille note takers and the KNFB Reader or KNFB Reader Mobile (for cell phones). Both of these tools use the latest technology to translate written text into Braille or a voice that reads printed material aloud. The KNFB Reader can even help a blind person read a menu or the instructions on a game.

Only a small percentage of blind people see nothing at all. CCTV magnifiers allow those with limited vision to read small print by projecting an enlarged version of the page onto a monitor. More advanced devices like ReadDesk can be attached to a computer or laptop. They magnify text, read it aloud, or convert it to an MP3 file.

Video games – How can a blind child or teenager play video games when all the action is visual? Games with audio cues and vibrations allow those who can't see the graphics to enjoy gaming. The technology is expensive, but soon it might be possible for a blind teenager to play Rock Band with his sighted friends.

Recreation – Balls with bells and high-pitched beeps make it possible for blind kids to participate in PE or just have fun playing sports. Some blind people are able to join baseball teams through the National Beep Ball Association. They even have a Beep Ball World Series!

Navigation – Your parents might have a GPS to help them avoid getting lost, but did you know this system can also help blind people travel independently? Another invention called the Ultracane sends out ultrasonic waves, similar to Mike's echolocation technique. A blind college student installed the Ultracane on his mountain bike. His handlebars vibrate to warn him of obstacles.

Will blind people be able to drive someday? In February, 2011, a blind man named Mark Riccobono drove a Ford Escape around the track at the Daytona International Speedway. This Blind Driver Challenge demonstrated technology that could make it possible for a person with little or no vision to drive a car. Two years later, Dan Parker, took a motocycle on a two-mile ride at the Bonneville Salt Flats. He built the three-wheeler himself and installed it with a GPS.

These creative inventions show us that there are no limits to what a blind person can do if he or she wants to try. For more information on technology for the blind, visit the National Federation for the Blind's website: www.nfb.org.

THANK YOU

Mike: I first want to express my love, gratitude, and thanks to my wife, Karen who is my rock and who makes so many things possible for me with her wisdom and wit. Thanks also to Jeanette Hanscome for tirelessly writing, changing, and perfecting our collaborative effort, which finally is in your hands to read.

A special thanks to Susy Flory who started it all in 2010 by helping me to create *Thunder Dog* and connecting me with Jeanette. Chip MacGregor, thanks for being the best agent anyone could have and for keeping all our feet on the right path.

A very special thanks to Todd Jurek, Roselle's trainer and the best guide dog instructor in the business.

Next, I want to thank Dick Herboldsheimer, who taught me geometry in high school and who has been my friend and sometimes mentor ever since.

I also want to thank the staff, volunteers, and supporters of Guide Dogs for the Blind for creating such a wonderful training environment for people and dogs.

Finally, I want to express my thanks to the late Dr. Fred Reines, the discoverer of the neutrino and my academic advisor in college. Dr. Reines, you taught me to pay attention to the details. Observing the details saved my life on 9-11.

♥

Jeanette: I am so grateful to the many people who helped make this book possible. Thank you, Mike Hingson, for the honor of being part of this exciting project. I had so much fun writing about your amazing life.

Thank you to Susy Flory for pairing us up to write a book especially for kids. I deeply appreciate your constant support and help. I couldn't have done this without you.

To Kay Stern, Holly Cline, Charles Nathan, Todd Jurek, Susi Cherry, Warren and Claudia Wish, and members of the Carson City Guide Dogs Club: Thank you for answering endless questions about Roselle's puppy years and training, raising guide dog puppies, and life at Guide Dogs for the Blind. Your stories helped us bring Roselle to life.

Thank you, Andrea Sharaf, for all of your help with the editing process. You did a great job!

To my brave friend, Margo Reha, Thank you for allowing me to drive your car as research for "Campus, Cars, and Kidnappings." Our adventure in the Home Depot parking lot is one of my fondest memories of writing this book.

Finally, I want to thank our faithful Focus Group: Leslie Beasley; Amanda, Zack, Toby, and Michaela Brown; Anne, Brennan, and Bryan Pott; Cheri Bissett-Bouma and daughter Anja (Anja, if Roselle were here, she would want to give you a big doggie kiss.); Jill, Erica, and Zack Miller; Julie, Elizabeth, and Joe Parr; Christian and Nathan Hanscome; Frank and Beverly La Chapell; Kristy, Kai, and Devon Torrey; Sherry, Haley, and Dylan Farrell; Jen Grafton; Jenni, Joshua, Ruth, and Jeremiah Saake; Melanie Moen; Michelle and Rebekah Van Vliet; Rebecca, Jeremy, and Zachary Volkov; Renee, Gracie, and Graydon Johnson; Karen Hingson; Linda Shanks; and, Shane Gillespie. We can't express enough gratitude for your valuable feedback, encouragement and prayers, and for never giving up on this project.

If I left anyone out, please know I appreciate you!

ABOUT THE AUTHORS

Michael Hingson wrote the runaway bestseller, *Thunder Dog: The True Story of a Blind Man, His Guide Dog, and the Triumph of Trust at Ground Zero*. He lives on the water in Novato, California with his wife, Karen, his guide dog, Africa, and Africa's mother Fantasia. When he isn't traveling the world with Africa speaking and teaching, he enjoys playing with his dogs, cooking, and helping Karen with her quilting business. Mike's favorite things include Harry Potter books, nachos with cheese only, talking with people on his ham radio set, and listening to vintage radio shows. Visit Mike's website: www.michaelhingson.com.

Jeanette Hanscome is the author of three published books and many articles and stories. Her most recent work includes a ghostwritten story for Guideposts magazine and a chapter in *Rescue Dogs, Firefighting Heroes and Science Facts*. Though she has been visually impaired since birth, Jeanette refuses to allow her limitations to hold her back from doing the things she loves. When she isn't writing, she enjoys teaching writing workshops, knitting and crocheting, cooking and baking, reading, and spending time with family and friends. Visit Jeanette's website: www.jeanettehanscome.com.

87294358R00146

Made in the USA
Columbia, SC
14 January 2018